LET'S TALK

HUMAN HORIZONS SERIES

LET'S TALK

Learning language in everyday settings

Roy McConkey and Penny Price

A CONDOR BOOK
SOUVENIR PRESS (E & A) LTD

CONTENTS

ACKNOWLEDGEMENTS

We would like to say thanks to:

* Our colleagues in St Michael's House, Dublin and at the Macquarie University Special Education Centre, Sydney, for their participation in the research programmes which helped to clarify our thinking about the ideas expressed in this book..

* St Michael's House Research Committee, Macquarie University Research Committee, UNESCO, and the Apex Foundation for Research into Mental Retardation, for grants which have supported the research on which the book is based.

* Dr Barbara Stokes, chairperson of St Michael's House Research Committee and Professor James Ward, Professor of Special Education at Macquarie University, for their encouragement and support.

* Participants in the workshops held throughout Ireland in the autumn of 1984 to test the format of the book. We appreciated their honest reactions.

* Pat McConkey for typing the manuscript; Kate Flanagan and Penny Price for photographs and Dan O'Leary for the figures.

* The many parents and children who have worked with us and from whom we have learnt so much.

WELCOME

What this book is about

This book is about learning to talk—one of the most difficult tasks that young children have to master. Most of us cannot remember what it was like to be unable to talk because we have been doing it for so long. We cannot recall what it was like trying to make someone understand us before we could talk properly. We have forgotten the gestures and crude sounds we relied on then. But if you watch a young child, you will see how frustrating it can be—for child and adult alike—when, despite the child's best efforts, the adult fails to understand his message. Many children get upset, others become angry and some may simply give up trying.

What children need most at this stage is an adult, or adults, closely attuned to them. They need people who know their wants and the things they like best, who share their activities often enough to be able, almost always, to work out what it is that the children are trying to say. They depend on adults to interpret the world for them, to help them learn the words and sentences that will get their message across, and who will give them the incentive to move on to the next step in learning to talk.

This book is for all those adults who are interested in helping young children to learn to talk, or in helping them to talk better or to learn this difficult task a little faster than they might otherwise manage without extra help. There are many adults who fit this description; we hope that some or all of the following will find the book helpful.

Who can use this book?

The mother or father of a young child—perhaps your first
You will be interested in every aspect of your baby's development, including how he or she learns to talk, and you may want to know what you can do to help. You could be

in for a few surprises. You will discover that there is a lot more to talking than meets the eye—or should it be 'ear'? For example, we know from recent research that baby games, such as 'peek-a-boo' or 'pretending' with dolls and teddies, help children to get ready for talking.

We shall tell you about many other things that you could do to help children both before and after they start talking.

The parent of a child who is slow to talk
You may be worried in case something is seriously wrong with your son or daughter, yet your family, friends, perhaps even your doctor or health visitor, all tell you that there is nothing to be concerned about . . . 'Why, Einstein didn't talk until he was four.' But as one parent commented, Mrs Einstein probably worried about him, too!

We believe we can help you, mainly by suggesting things you can do that will help your child. First, we shall show you ways of discovering your child's strong points, as well as his or her weaknesses. Secondly, you will read about everyday activities around the home and neighbourhood that can be turned into learning experiences for your child. In many cases, if you follow the simple suggestions given in the book, you will soon begin to see your child progress, although possibly fairly slowly at first.

In some cases, however, slowness in learning to talk may be due to a more basic problem, such as hearing loss. All children who are slow to talk should have their hearing checked. This requires the specialist services of an audiologist. Your local doctor or health visitor will tell you where to obtain this vital facility.

There can be other reasons why some children have difficulty in learning to talk. You should consult a psychologist or speech therapist for advice. Again your health visitor will give you addresses or telephone numbers.

Perhaps you have a son or daughter with an obvious handicap
You may have realised for some time that talking will not come easily. Your child is probably receiving specialist help already, either from a teacher or a therapist. Yet you wonder if enough is being done by either of them or by yourself.

In our experience, the answer is nearly always that more could be done by both! In this book, we have chosen to write about what *parents could do*. Our approach is NOT to turn you into teachers or therapists—quite the opposite. We want you to continue doing the things you do best: caring for your child, playing and relaxing with him when you have time, and getting jobs done around the house. We will show you how you can use these times to give your child extra help in learning to talk. You will not need any special equipment, nor will you have to set aside special times each day when you and your child must not be interrupted. Better still, we shall describe activities that the whole family can join in, so that it is not all left to one person alone.

Notice we used the word *could*: the book tells you what you *could* do. You know your child better than anyone outside the family ever will, and this makes you the best person to decide both how much you do and which particular activities you will use with your child. You know what is best for you and your family, and how much you can fit in to your daily lives. It is

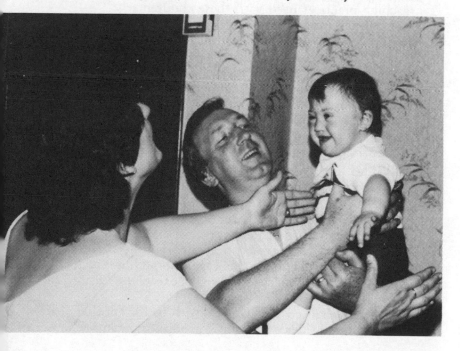

most important that both you and your child enjoy the activities you engage in, and that the atmosphere is relaxed. If you are feeling under pressure neither of you will benefit; wait until you have a little more time.

It is important to understand that some handicapped children are extremely slow in learning to talk. We describe in some detail the many skills that children have to acquire *before* you can expect them to talk. It can take some of them quite a while to master these, so there is plenty you can be doing to help. Do not be too disheartened if your child does not progress as fast as you would like.

Maybe you are a playgroup leader, teacher or therapist
You are on the look-out for new ideas because you know very well that language delays, speech disorders and communication problems are always cropping up, with as many as one in five pre-schoolers affected in some way or other.

You will find our approach quite different from the many language kits currently available, or from the traditional teaching practices used with these children.

Instead of prescribing special teaching activities, we have chosen to focus on helping teachers to identify suitable *learning targets* for each individual child and showing how these can be realised in a wide range of situations.

We do not see ourselves in competition with other approaches. It is too simple a question to ask which way is best. Rather, we passionately believe that the specialist methods commonly used *must* be complemented by an *everyday* dimension, in order to ensure that the children's mastery of new skills is embedded into their daily routines and is not something learnt in special settings with special equipment which they are unable to use in their everyday lives.

If you have experienced the frustration of seeing children perform well during the teaching sessions, yet fail to show the same skills in everyday settings, then you need to read this book. It should make you think again about how much of your energy you devote to 'special' language teaching sessions and it will show you that there *is* another way.

We are delighted to have you with us for another reason. You might consider organising a group for parents who want

to work through the book together in the form of a workshop or course. This will benefit many parents who may not otherwise have the confidence to work from a book on their own.

We have prepared a series of video-programmes to accompany the book. There are five programmes in all, one each covering Sections Two to Six respectively. They are in colour and each one lasts around 20 minutes. All the children taking part are developmentally-delayed and they are filmed mostly at home with their families.

Further information about the programmes can be obtained from the address on p. 38. A workshop course could be built around the programmes.

A nurse or care-giver of children living in residential homes
We have a special word of welcome for you. We know that you are kept very busy and it is not easy for you to find time to 'chat' or to play with the children. Yet we believe that you are in the best position to give the children in your care the help they most need with learning to communicate and to talk. It should not mean *extra* work for you; rather we shall describe

how you can further the chidren's learning in the course of your normal duties. It helps, too, if you are working regularly with the same group of children. Our approach should not cause the bad feelings that sometimes arise between staff in residential and educational services.

Anyone interested in young children and early language
We hope the book lives up to your expectations. If we succeed in sharing with you the fascinating story of how children learn to talk and how best adults can help, then we shall be satisfied.

How to use this book
We presume that the people reading the book are mostly mothers and fathers, but these terms should be taken to include all adults. In addition, we often refer to the child as 'your child'. However, the ideas can be used with all children of similar abilities, they are not just for one particular child.

We had a problem with the use of the words 'he' or 'she'. It is confusing to change from one to the other and cumbersome to use both each time, so we decided to use the term 'he', mainly because more boys than girls experience problems in learning to talk. But if you have a daughter, please read 'he' as 'she' and accept our apologies in advance.

We realise that you are eager to start doing something with your child. Perhaps you do not like reading or begrudge the time spent on it. If so, you are exactly the sort of people we had in mind. 'On your marks, get set, go!' sums up the style of this book.

| ON YOUR MARKS | The first pages of each section in the book describe the topics covered in that part. We also explain why they are important in children's development and we provide the reasons for the advice given later on.

| GET SET | The middle pages of each section describe the steps we advise you to take before you start doing *new* things with your child. Mostly they involve you in closely watching your child for a day or two. We suggest, too, that you keep a simple record of what he does, so that you can look back over it and think about what to do next. From here, we shall guide you

to the activities that are most likely to be appropriate for your child.

The 'get set' pages have a dotted line down the outside edge, so that you can find them easily.

GO These pages contain suggested activities that you can use to further your child's development of the skills needed in communication and talking. Sometimes the same activities occur in one or more sections. This is quite deliberate because often the best activities are those which nurture various skills.

The 'go' pages have a solid line down the outside edge.

A quick flick through the pages will let you spot the different parts:

No line	*'On your marks'*	Background descriptions and explanations
Dotted line	*'Get set'*	Observation activities
Solid line	*'Go'*	Activities to help your child

Planning your reading

YOU DO NOT NEED TO READ THE BOOK FROM COVER TO COVER although you may want to, in order to get a comprehensive picture of what is involved in learning to talk from the time a baby is born through to the point where he is talking in sentences and communicating with people outside his immediate family and the home setting. Rather, the book is designed to let you slip from one part to the next. You can read only those parts that most apply to you at present.

Here are four examples of different ways in which you can use the book, depending upon your immediate needs.

1 *Explanations.* For some people, understanding *why* a particular line of action is recommended is very important. They want to know all that's involved in learning to talk and why some children find it difficult. They want a reason before doing anything. The *on your marks* parts of each section provide the foundation of knowledge on which the observation tasks and recommended activities are based. Together they form a mini-textbook on children's language and communication.

2   *'One topic at a time'.*   Some people prefer to deal with one topic in depth—background description and explanations, observation tasks, and activities to encourage progress. These people should go to the section that seems most suited to their children's needs and work through the *on your marks, get set* and *go* pages. This procedure can be followed with each section, as it becomes appropriate for their child's needs. It is a good method to use when a group of people are working through the book together (see p. 37).

3   *'What can my child do?'*   Many parents are very anxious to find out precisely what their child can and cannot do. The *get set* pages (those with dotted lines) will therefore appeal to them. Here the special forms and charts will clearly tell them what they want to know. From here they can go on to read the *go* pages, starting at the level which, for their child, represents the next step in learning to talk.

This plan should appeal particularly to staff working with a group of children, each with differing problems at different levels.

4   *'Desperate for new activities'.*   Some parents may feel that, since they spend a lot of time with their children, they want suggestions for new games and activities to include in their routines. These can be found in the *go* pages of each section (those with solid lines on the outside edge). However, we strongly advise that you look at the *get set* pages of whichever section is appropriate for your child. You can then be sure that the activities you are doing are the right ones for his language learning level.

After looking through the contents of the book and familiarising yourself with the way it is organised, use it in whatever way best suits your needs. It may be one of the ways we have just described, or you may have worked out a plan of your own. Our hope is that you will come to understand more about the problem of helping your child learn to talk, that you will be better at observing what he can do now and that you will learn ways of extending his language and communication skills.

SECTION ONE: WHAT'S INVOLVED IN LEARNING TO TALK?

Talking is one of the most difficult skills young children have to master. This section will explain why that is so and will outline some of the problems that children encounter.

As we mentioned earlier, this section is divided into three parts:

ON YOUR MARKS

Talking is a combination of skills. Talking involves speech, language and communication. We tell you about each, especially the differences between them. It is important for adults to understand how they differ when it comes to helping young children learn to talk.

GET SET

Hearing loss—the invisible handicap. Children need to hear clearly in order to pick up language and to speak distinctly. Here we describe how you can check your child's hearing and what you can do to ensure that he hears you, even if he has some difficulty in hearing.

GO

A guide to the book. We explain how the rest of the book is organised and how you can find your way through it. We also suggest ways of getting help from other parents and specialist staff as you work through the book. Details are given of special video-programmes which are available to supplement the material in the book.

| ON YOUR MARKS |

TALKING IS A COMBINATION OF SKILLS

Can you imagine a glass of Irish Coffee sitting in front of you? No? Why not make yourself one? You need hot, black coffee, three teaspoonfuls of brown sugar and some Irish whisky. Mix them together and then float cream on the top in a thick layer. A rather delicious combination.

As you drink it, you do not notice the separate ingredients. Indeed, they are so mixed up, that you could not separate them even if you wanted to.

So what has Irish Coffee got to do with children learning to talk? Let us explain. You are good at talking; you can chat away to your friends without having to think about what you are doing—especially after a few Irish Coffees! Talking, like walking or eating, is just another well-practised skill—right? No—that's wrong. Talking is not *one* skill; it is actually a mixture of different ingredients, like Irish Coffee. Adults are so used to mixing them that they forget the separate elements that go into talking.

Imagine a wife saying to her husband, 'I'd love a cup of tea.' A short, simple sentence. But look at all it involves.

SPEECH—The wife produces the sounds by moving her lips, tongue, etc. She can speak softly or loudly and may talk with an Irish or Australian accent.

LANGUAGE—She speaks in English, although she could have used French or Greek or any other language her husband understands. She has to remember the right words to use and put them in the correct order.

COMMUNICATION—She wants to tell her husband to make the tea. She said it rather indirectly, but no doubt he got the message. If he didn't respond, she might have gone on to say, 'Is it your turn to make it?' or, 'Get up off your backside and make the tea!'

THOUGHTS—Her thoughts might have been something like:

I'm thirsty; it's nearly bed-time; coffee keeps me awake. When all these ideas came together, she expressed them as, 'I'd love a cup of tea'.

Did you realise there was so much to talking? Probably not; but then you have had at least 20 years' practice at mixing these four ingredients. It is no wonder they seem like the one skill—which we call talking. It is not so easy for young children, though. They have to cope with mastering the separate ingredients as well as learning how to mix them correctly. Not surprisingly, they prefer to practise one thing at a time. That's why you often come across young babies doing the following:

* They communicate without speaking or using a language.
* They speak but without using proper words.
* They pick up the meaning of their parents' language, without speaking or communicating.
* And they can think without saying a word!

It is a pity adults do not remember learning to talk.If we did, we might begin to see the children's difficulties. For instance, are you convinced that thoughts, speech, language and communication are really all that different? Can you have one without the other?

Can you THINK without speaking?   Try to recall being at the seaside on a warm summer's day. Perhaps you went swimming or paddling in the water . . . or played a game with the children . . . or read a book or magazine . . . had a picnic lunch. Imagine it now. That is one example of thinking without words, although you could describe your thoughts if we asked you to.

Here is another example. Which way do screws go into wood—clockwise or anticlockwise? Now be honest—did you have to twist your hand to remember? That's another way we can think without words.

Although we cannot be sure, it appears that babies think by recalling actions and images. Only later do they put words to these thoughts or, as we say, 'talk to themselves'!

Can you COMMUNICATE without speaking? That's an easier one. Babies certainly can. They cry when they want to be fed, changed or cuddled, and mothers gradually come to recognise what each cry means. Later the infant may point, shake his head or wave his arms and you do not have to be his parent to get the message.

Adults sometimes use these signs if they are talking to young children or if they are shopping in a foreign country and do not know the language. Have you ever done this? Gesturing can be frustrating. Misunderstandings arise easily and you feel embarrassed. Still, they do work, as long as your message is simple. But try miming 'the customer is always right' and see how far you get!

Can you SPEAK without knowing a language? Yes, you can; although you do not often do so. For example, say out loud this sentence: 'Momo defan wampadu sumta.'

You are unlikely to know this language—indeed these could be the worst swear words, for all you know—yet you are quite able to speak them. This happens to children, too, although they do not read the words; instead, they copy what you say. You may think they have learnt the words, but have they?

Imagine you are being shown a picture book about Cinderella by a native African speaker. She says, 'Momo defan wampadu sumta'—you copy her. She turns the page. 'Defan jola wampan ciklik ba,' and you say that, too.

Although you can speak the words, you do not know what each one means. You have not learnt the language. Likewise with children:

ADULT: Cinders is very sad.
CHILD: Cinders is very sad.
ADULT: She's crying because she's lonely.
CHILD: 'Cause she's lonely.
ADULT: That's right and here's her wicked step-mother.
CHILD: Wicked step-mother.
ADULT: Who is it?
CHILD: Wicked step-mother.

The child *appears to know* the language, but because he is only imitating us or answering questions, we can't be sure.

Can you learn LANGUAGE without speaking?   Beware—the answer will surprise you. Children can learn a language without saying a word. This is hard for adults to appreciate. To them, a new language is learnt by speaking it. But that's not how you learned your first language. You did it by watching and listening to what was going on around you and puzzling out what the different words meant.

Imagine you are an African toddler. Your mother points to a picture of a duck swimming in a pool surrounded by tall grass and says, 'Defan.' You look a little puzzled, so she points up to the sky. 'Defan,' she says again, and then she grips part of her dress and says, 'Defan,' as she points to it. Have you puzzled out what 'defan' means? Is it *duck*? It could be . . . if there were ducks flying in the sky and on the pattern of mother's dress. Or 'defan' could be the word for *bird*. After all, young children sometimes call all animals 'doggie'. But 'defan' doesn't mean 'duck' or 'bird'. Do you want more clues? Mother brings out a handkerchief, a tennis ball and a sheet off the bed and says they're all 'defan'! Confused? 'Defan' means 'white'. Mother had pointed out all the white things . . . clouds, dress, and so forth.

Because you already know a language, you can translate one word (defan) for another (white). Babies cannot do this. They have to puzzle out the connection between the sound they hear their parents use and what it means. They have to *listen*, *watch* and *think*. If they have an idea of its meaning they will have a go at using it. 'Yellow?' 'No,' says mum, 'that's not yellow, it's white.'

Puzzling out what adults are talking about can be a difficult job for babies. Think how you would feel in a foreign country where no one spoke your language. What should people do to help you understand their speech?

1   They should make clear
    what they were talking
    about—by pointing or
    using gestures, such as
    pretending to drink when
    talking about drink.
2   They should choose com-
    monly used words or
    words that you would
    need to use.
3   They should talk in short,
    simple sentences.
4   They should give you
    time to watch, listen and
    think about the meaning
    of the words. You would
    not need to talk to under-
    stand them.

These are precisely the same four factors that help children
to learn their native language. Even so, it usually takes them
all of four years to master the basics. Perhaps you now see
why!

You can understand, too, why we urge parents to *ignore* the
usual advice to 'do lots of talking to the child'. It is not how
much you say that is vital, but *what* you say.

Helping children learn

Although we have stressed the differences between speech,
language, communication and thinking, children do not learn
them separately. Indeed, good talkers are those who can mix
them easily and fluently. So what can parents, family and
teachers do to help? After years of research, there are three
ways we can be sure of:

1   *Doing* things together with the child. The adult and one child share the same activity, be it a game, 'housework', an outing or a cuddle. This should happen regularly.

2   Encouraging the child to *communicate*, by responding to his attempts and by giving him choices.

3   By talking about what the child is doing or is interested in. You need to take *your lead from the child*.

We're already doing that! That is what most parents say and it is nearly always true. Parents are the people who give their child most help in learning to talk; they are the people who are with the child most and who best know his likes and dislikes. This is still true even when the children are also getting help from specialists, such as therapists or teachers. Thus, we want to say to you, keep on with the good work. You are on the right lines.

But we suspect that you want to do more. Perhaps you feel that your efforts are not enough and you are disheartened that your child is not progressing faster. Please think over the following:

* *Maybe your expectations are too high.* Talking does not come suddenly or easily. There are many other things that children have to learn before they start talking, such as understanding objects and events (see Section Three). Perhaps you should concentrate more on these, rather than trying to get your child to speak.

* *Maybe you need to tune in better to your child's level.* We will show you how to do this later in the book.

* *Maybe you need more variety in what you do.* We have plenty of suggestions for activities you may not have tried before.

* *Maybe you are not doing what you think you are doing.* In our anxiety to help children, we can sometimes make things more difficult for them. We will show you some common mistakes adults make.

* *Maybe your child needs more time.* Some children take longer than others to learn. We do not know why it should be but it happens so often, we think of it as normal. If you have done all you can, then think of your child as a slow starter who may well catch up or make faster progress in the future.

Summary
By now you should have a better idea of why talking is so much more complicated than many other things that children have to learn. Talking involves:
* thinking
* communication
* mastering a language
* speaking.

And children have to be able to do all four at the *same time*. Talk is too small a word for it: it is human communication. Ready for another Irish Coffee after all that?

GET SET

HEARING LOSS—THE INVISIBLE HANDICAP

'Nature which gave us two eyes and two ears to hear has given us but one tongue to speak.' Jonathan Swift put talking in its rightful place. Certainly for children, seeing and hearing are more vital in learning to talk than moving their tongues to produce sounds. We have given you the reasons in the previous pages. Now we want to describe how you can check if your child has any difficulties, particularly in hearing, that could get in his way when learning to talk.

Children likely to have hearing problems

It is assumed that all children can hear. Yet as many as one in ten will have poor hearing. With some only one ear is affected and, for others, the deafness will come and go due to infections. But one in fifty children will have such a severe loss that they require special help.

Some children are particularly prone to hearing problems. There may be a history of deafness in the family and this can be passed on to the child through the genes inherited from the parents, even though the mother and father have no problems in hearing. This is more likely to happen with boys than with girls.

Rubella babies (those whose mothers had German measles in the early stages of pregnancy) are also likely to have impaired hearing, along with other handicaps.

Children with Down's Syndrome are also very prone to hearing difficulties. It may be as many as two in every three. In the past, these problems were not recognised. The signs of hearing loss were thought to be features of their mental handicap. Yet if appropriate action is taken, their hearing loss can be reduced. They will be better able to learn language and to talk more clearly.

How do you know if a child has a hearing loss?

Complete deafness is very rare. Rather, it is better to think in terms of a *loss of hearing* that can range from mild to severe. But even at its worst, some noises still get through. This means it can be hard to know for sure whether a child—particularly a young baby—has a hearing loss. One 'test' is not enough. As in a detective story, the evidence has to build up until there is enough to convict.

Infants with marked loss of hearing can *appear* to be hearing quite well. For example, the baby is asleep in his cot for an afternoon nap. His mother goes in to waken him. She pulls back the curtains, walks over and leans on his cot and calls his name. He wriggles, opens his eyes and smiles. He woke when his mum called him. Or did he? He could have been wakened by:

* the *brightness* as she pulled back the curtains;
* the *movements* (vibrations) as she walked across the room and touched his cot, or
* he may have sensed her *smell* in the room.

All these were clues to the mother's presence and the child did not need to hear, although it appeared to the mother that he had heard her.

If you want to test your child's ability to hear, you have to get rid of these other clues. When you go to wake him, you will not pull the curtains or put on the light; you will not touch the cot or go to the baby. Instead, you will stand about five feet away and call him—softly at first, then more loudly if need be. If the child *stirs*, then you can be confident that he heard your sounds. But what if he does not wake up? Does that mean that he is deaf? Not at all. He could be a heavy sleeper. You need more evidence.

It is better to 'test' when your child is awake and alert. Remember, you must still be sure that your child is responding to sound, not to what he sees, or to movement, or to smell. Here are some ideas:

1 Your baby is lying contentedly in his pram, cot or bouncing chair. Without letting him see you, start talking as you would if you were facing him, but not loudly. Does he become active, maybe even smile in anticipation of seeing you?
2 If your child is becoming restless and whining in his cot, pram or chair and you come up quietly behind him and start talking in your usual way but *without* him seeing you—does that quieten him?

3   Your child is lying on his side on the floor, playing with a toy. Kneel down quietly about four or five feet from him and softly call his name. Does he try and turn over to see where you are? Do you have to talk loudly before he does? Later, you could try him on his other side to test his hearing in the other ear.

4   If your child can easily turn his head when sitting upright on your knee, you can try this 'test'. This is known as a 'distraction' test and is the one used by health visitors, public health nurses and doctors to screen babies' hearing. Ideally, it requires three adults but you can get by with two.

In a quiet room, mum has the baby on her knee and they are looking at a book or toy. Dad stands behind them and to one side, about six feet away, and softly calls the child by name. If he looks round then he has heard dad calling him. Mum gets the child interested in the book again and dad quietly moves to the other side to test the child's hearing in

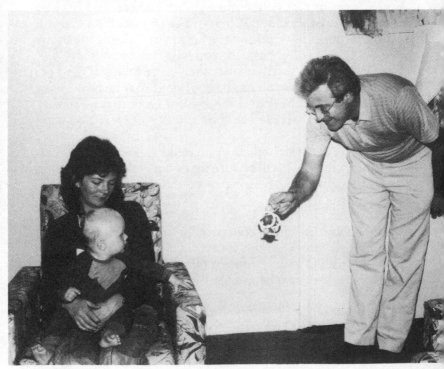

the other ear. Again, the child should turn to the sound. You may notice a child always turns to the same side, even though the noise comes from different sides. This can be a sign that he is not hearing very well in one ear. He always turns to the side of his good ear because that is where he hears the sound coming from.

This test is not foolproof. Some children with hearing losses seem to hear, but they get a clue from dad's movements or see him out of the corner of their eye, or they think it is some new game and keep looking from side-to-side.

Conversely, children with good hearing may appear to have a problem. They may be so engrossed in the book or toy that they fail to turn when called. They may be so used to living in noisy surroundings that they cannot be distracted by sounds, or they may not be interested in the particular noises you make. Hence, don't rely on one test; keep checking over a period of time.

Is he hearing some sounds but not others?

The sounds we make when talking vary a great deal. For example, say 'oo' (as in 'shoe') and then say 'sss' by blowing *gently* through your teeth. Notice the difference. It is possible for children to hear one sort of sound—the lower vowel sounds—rather than the higher, consonant-type sounds. This type of hearing problem means that the child picks up only parts of what is said to him, no matter how loudly you talk. For instance, he hears 'Where's daddy?' as '—er— —a—y?'

You might try using two different sounds—'oo' and 'ss'—during the 'tests' we described above and note your child's reactions to each.

Children's hearing can be affected by minor illnesses

Children with normal hearing can become 'deaf' for a week or so at a time. This can happen when they have a heavy cold or some other infection at the back of the nose or top of the throat, or if they suffer from catarrh. Some handicapped children seem particularly prone to these problems. In severe cases fluid may gather in their middle ear, making it all the harder for the children to hear.

Your doctor may be able to prescribe a course of medicine that clears up the problem. Other children may need a simple operation to clear the fluid from the ear or to remove adenoids, if they are enlarged.

If your child is prone to any of the above problems, it is worth keeping a check on his hearing from time to time, so that you know when he is not hearing well.

Hearing assessments

In most districts, babies can have their hearing checked in the clinic when they are between six and 12 months old. We advise all parents to take their babies along for these check-ups. If you have not been, or if you have never been asked to take your baby for a check-up, then call into the clinic and ask for an appointment.

If you are worried about your child's hearing you can ask your GP to refer you to a specialist centre, where a full examination will be carried out. Do not be worried that the specialist will be annoyed if your child's hearing is normal. He or she much prefers to show parents that their child can hear, or to reassure them that any problem will clear up quickly, rather than see a child for the first time when he is three, who is not talking because of a hearing loss that should have been detected earlier. These are also the people who will advise whether or not your child can benefit from a hearing aid.

CONTACT: 1   Health Visitor or Public Health Nurse at the clinic for a hearing check-up.

2   Your GP for referral to specialists who test children's hearing (they are called *audiologists*).

What you can do

1   Keep a check on your child's hearing.
2   Remember to:
  * *talk softly*. Children with hearing loss can still react to loud noises;
  * *check both ears*. The child may have poor hearing in one ear and not in the other;
  * *check for different sorts of sounds*. The child may hear low ('oo') sounds but not high ('sss') sounds;

* *ensure the child is only reacting to sound.* And not to what he sees, movements he feels or to new smells, such as perfumes, etc;
* *ensure the child can react to sound.* That he is not so engrossed in his play that he does not want to look round, and that he is able to move freely (not always possible if his motor control is poor).

After trying to check your child's hearing, you might make some notes in the spaces below:

My child's hearing appears to be all right because—

My child might have some loss of hearing because—

If your child has a hearing loss
The sooner you and the family know, the better. There are specialists available to give you advice and, if your child would benefit from a hearing aid—not all children do—then they will arrange for this.

More important is the way you and the family talk to the child. Remember, your child has a hearing loss, he is not deaf. Hence, you need to make it easier for him to hear by:
* Facing him when talking.
* Getting down to his level, so that you are face-to-face.
* Being close to him—three feet or so.
* Talking distinctly but in a normal way. There is no need to shout or exaggerate.
* Cutting down background noises that might get in the way—radio, TV, etc.
* Trying to understand what he says or what he is telling you by gestures. Take your cue from what interests him.
* Getting your message across by showing (e.g. holding out an object (or miming an action) as well as by talking.

These points are also of help with children who are prone to temporary hearing losses, due to colds, catarrh, etc. Indeed, *all children who are learning to talk would benefit from them.*

This book is NOT specifically about children with hearing problems (we mention some books that are on page 248). If you are already in contact with specialists because of your child's hearing difficulties, be guided by their advice. You should find this book useful, provided you adapt our suggestions to accord with your child's needs.

Other handicaps

There are other handicaps that make it difficult for children to speak. These are usually more obvious than hearing problems —cleft palate and lip and cerebral palsy—and you have probably had some specialist help already. If not, ask your Health Visitor or Public Health Nurse, or your GP, to refer you to a speech therapist. Although this book does not deal specifically with the problems these children face, many of our ideas can apply to them, so long as they also receive the specialist attention they usually need.

Most mentally handicapped children are slow at learning to talk. Sometimes they have other specific problems, like a hearing loss, and these must be attended to. However, this book is very appropriate for children who are mentally handicapped. It is vital that the specialist work of teachers and therapists is balanced by extending the child's learning into everyday activities. In our experience, parents are the best people to do this. Indeed, most of our work is with parents of mentally handicapped children and the ideas contained in this book have evolved from these experiences. (If your child has none of these handicaps and yet is still very slow at learning to talk, ask your GP or your Health Visitor or Public Health Nurse to refer you to a psychologist.)

GO

A GUIDE TO THE BOOK
There are six sections to the book after this one. (See Fig. 2.)
As you can see, they start and end at different points on the age
span between birth and 36 months. However, these ages are

PREVERBAL → VERBAL

SECTION 2: GET THE MESSAGE ?

SECTION 3: NOW I UNDERSTAND

SECTION 4 : TAKING TURNS

SECTION 5: THERE'S A WORD FOR IT

SECTION 6: MAKING SENSE OF SENTENCES

SECTION 7 : LISTEN WHO'S TALKING

0   12   24   36 MONTHS

ROUGH AGES OF CHILDREN

only a rough guide. We prefer to think in terms of a continuum from preverbal to verbal abilities.

* If your child is *not* talking ('preverbal') then Sections Two, Three, Four and Seven are the ones most suitable for you.

* If your child *is talking*, knows quite a few words and even says some short sentences, then Sections Two, Five, Six and Seven are the ones for you.

* If your child is *just starting* to talk, you will find something of interest to you in all six sections.

Children continue to learn beyond the range we are concerned with here. We had to draw the line somewhere, otherwise this would have been a very long book. We opted to concentrate on the *foundation skills*. Once children have acquired these, they develop their own momentum in mastering the finer aspects of speech, language and communication.

At the end of Section Six, we shall give you some pointers as to what these are (p. 224). However, the dotted ends in the diagram are a reminder that development can continue in all areas.

There is one other thing we want you to remember. The six sections are not separate, as Fig. 2 suggests; that merely shows you how the book is arranged.

In terms of how it is with children, you should think of the cylinders as a bunch of straws held within a fist. If you cut off the tops and looked down, you would see a pattern something like the one shown in Fig. 3.

Communication is at the heart of the book. That is what talking is all about—sharing your experiences, feelings, ideas and wants with other people.

The four circles—representing *Taking Turns*, *Understanding*, *Words* and *Sentences*—are all inter-linked. They overlap and, when taken together, make communication possible. However, they all have their own distinct features as well and, although you will find some repetition from section to section, there is much that is new in each one.

Finally, the child is surrounded by *adult conversation*. Adults can affect children's learning by what they do and say

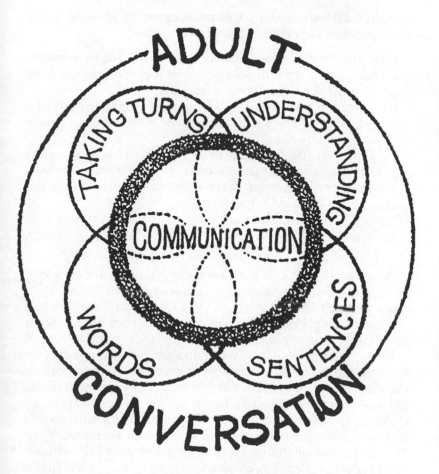

and this embraces all five aspects involved—from communication to sentences.

Unclear speech

We should warn you that this book is not about helping children to speak clearly. We are not concerned with the way children speak; rather, our emphasis is on what they say (language) and why they say it (communication).

Clear speech requires careful movements of the tongue and lips, combined with controlled breathing. For instance, as you say the word 'basketball', think of what is going on in your mouth. Children need a lot of practice before they can make these rapid movements. They get this when:

* they are eating, especially chewing hard, crumbly foods. Children who are still on a bottle or soft food do not have good control of their tongue and lips.
* they attempt to say words. The more words they know the better, because this forces them to be more precise in their pronunciation—'bat', 'bad', 'bag'.
* they put words together in sentences. This gives them practice in sequences of movements. Even adults can have difficulty with some of these—'She sells sea-shells on the sea-shore'. Practice helps, however.
* strangers fail to understand what they are saying and they have to repeat themselves. This forces them to attempt better efforts.

When you know a child well you can make out things he says more easily than strangers can. You are tuned in to his way of talking. As children talk to people outside the family—their playmates, neighbours, playgroup leaders—they have to learn to talk more clearly if they want to be understood.

Once children have become competent communicators who know the basics of their language, then you can start to work on the clarity of their speech. But by this time, you probably will not need to: they may have begun to improve anyway. Some children, however, do experience extra problems with speech and would benefit from the help of a speech therapist. Your Health Visitor or Public Health Nurse, or your GP, will put you in touch. Of course, children with poor hearing will find it very difficult to talk clearly. You have to accept the best they can do.

Sign language

With children who are very slow to develop speech or whose speech is very indistinct, many specialists now recommend that they learn a sign system to help them to communicate. This can be a stepping stone for some children on the road to talking; it does not mean that they will never speak. The sign systems are often based on hand signs used by deaf people. Systems vary from country to country. In Britain and

Australia, a system known as *Makaton* is popular, whereas another called *Lamh* is used throughout the Irish Republic. In the United States, an adaptation of American Indian signs is used called *AmerInd*. All were designed with mentally handicapped people in mind.

  * If your child is already using signs, this book will still be of use to you.
  * If you are interested in knowing more about sign systems, talk to a speech therapist or teacher.

Don't walk alone

One last word before you start. It is not easy to put into practice what you read about in a book. Ideas that sound good on paper may just fizzle out in reality. The result is that you become discouraged and stop trying new things. So try not to walk alone. Before you begin, we want you to think about doing some of the following:

Tell the family—Talk about the book with your husband or wife or other adults living in your house. Let them know what it is about and what you will be doing. Involve your other children in this; even the little ones will enjoy looking at the photographs in the book and hearing you explain what they mean.

Meet a friend—If you have a friend who is very interested in your child or who has a child similar to yours, then get them involved, too. Two minds are better than one and sharing the load usually lightens it.

Ask at the clinic—Do not be afraid of asking for advice from professionals who are in contact with your child—playgroup leaders, psychologists, teachers, speech therapists. Tell them what you are aiming to do and, if you encounter any problems or if you are unsure what to do next, ask them if they have any suggestions.

Parent groups—In our experience, parents can learn a lot from other parents, especially those whose children are experiencing, or have experienced, the same problems. You may have received this book through a group of parents organised by someone in your area. But for those not so lucky, you might think of getting together a self-help group. Put up a notice at the local clinic or hospital, contact voluntary societies organised by parents (see your local Telephone Directory), ask at your child's nursery or school, or contact your Health Visitor or Public Health Nurse to see if she knows anyone.

If a group of you can get together, this will give you a chance to pick each others' brains for ideas. Most of all, you will probably find the group a source of encouragement. There will be times when you are getting nowhere, but if you can talk to someone, then it will seem less hopeless than you thought. Equally, there will be times when other people could do with your help.

Video—We have made a series of video-programmes which show many of our suggestions being used at home by mothers, fathers, brothers and sisters. All the children in the video who are learning to talk are mentally handicapped, but the ideas are applicable to any child.

You might find it helpful to see our ideas in action; pictures do speak louder than words. It is especially helpful to view the programmes over a number of weeks with other parents, trying out some of the ideas between sessions and then discussing how you got on.

The programmes are in colour and last around two hours in total. They can be purchased in either VHS or Beta format.

Further details can be obtained from: St Michael's House, 'Videocourses', Upper Kilmacud Road, Stillorgan, Co Dublin, Republic of Ireland.

The future
Finally: keep the book safe. Parts of it may be too advanced for your child at present, but in six months' time you might discover that certain sections are very relevant to you because your child has come on so much.

We recommend that you take down the book from time-to-time and read over the parts that you had skipped previously. We see the book as an investment for the future, as well as a help to you now.

SECTION TWO: GET THE MESSAGE?

If your child cries and you have to have to guess what the trouble is . . .

Or if he turns his head away and closes his mouth tight every time you offer him custard . . .

Or if he jumps up and down and points outside, while you rack your brains wondering what he means, then this section is for you. Read on.

What you will read about in this section

ON YOUR MARKS

1 *What is communication?* At the earliest stage, it consists of unintentional messages sent by the child, to which his mother or father respond by trying to find out what the child wants—they learn to read his messages and respond appropriately. Only later does the child start to send intentional messages.

2 *How communication develops.* It grows out of an infant's need to have adults do things for him and his desire to influence the people, objects and events in his environment. The best teacher is a responsive adult who is closely tuned in to the child's early attempts at communicating.

3 *The form of early communication.* Babies and young infants cannot send messages by words in the way adults can. Instead, they use gestures and vocalisations which are global and gross to begin with—cries or wriggles—but their methods become more and more precise as they mature and their sounds merge into words.

4 *The range of early messages.* Children learn to send a variety of messages, such as making *demands* ('I want' . . . an object, attention or something to happen); *refusing* when they do not want something; *greeting* people when they come and go; *commenting* by means of indicating, describing or giving

information; and they *ask* and *answer* questions. We shall explain these different messages in detail.

GET SET

5 *Your child's communications.* We shall describe how you can pick up the messages your child is sending; how to record on special forms both what they *do* and *say* and what you think they *mean*.

GO

6 *Encouraging communication.* We suggest ways of encouraging your child, a) to communicate *more often* (and not just in particular situations and with certain people), b) to communicate *more widely*—by introducing new types of messages that he may not at present be using and c) to communicate *more precisely*—by making more specific gestures or sounds.

| ON YOUR MARKS |

WHAT IS COMMUNICATION?

'Hello, Daddy! I want a biscuit. Look at my teddy bear! Will you play ball with me? It's a big red ball! What's that?'

By the time a child can say sentences like these, adults have no trouble working out what 'messages' he is sending. We can react immediately to each 'message' in whatever way is appropriate. Communication is smooth and easy. For example, in response to what the child said above, Dad can give a greeting as he walks in at the door, take the biscuit jar down from the shelf and offer it to the child, stop to look at teddy, or to play a game of ball, agree that it *is* 'a big red ball' and answer one of the many questions that young children ask about the things we are doing, and the objects we are doing them with.

But *how* does the child learn to send so many different sorts of messages, and when does he begin this complicated task? How do we, as adults, know what the child is trying to say before he uses clear words?

The answer to these questions may surprise you. *Communication* does not suddenly start when the child begins to talk; it has been taking place from the moment he was born. Often the child and the adult may be quite unconscious that what they are doing is *communicating*. Yet this is the earliest stage in the long and sometimes difficult process of learning to talk. The infant is not sending *intentional* messages, and his early 'messages' are very limited in variety—non-specific crying which could indicate a need for food or comfort or relief from pain. But the mother, or care-giver, responds to this early, unclear message by trying to find out what the child wants. Is he hungry, wet, cold, pricked by a safety pin or plagued by a pain in his tummy? Once she has discovered the trouble and responded appropriately, peace is restored.

Babies also learn to coo and smile, as well as to cry, and once again the mother responds to the child's *unintentional* communication as if he were trying to say, 'Hello! I'm really pleased to see you!' A little later he will wave his arms around and gaze at anything in his line of vision, and his mother will *respond* by touching the little row of ducks attached to his cot,

or the coloured mobile hanging from the ceiling and say, 'See
the ducks!' In each instance the child's behaviour is *unintentional*
but the mother *responds* as if he has been trying to give her a
clear message:
* I'm hungry.
* I'm pleased to see you.
* Look at the ducks!

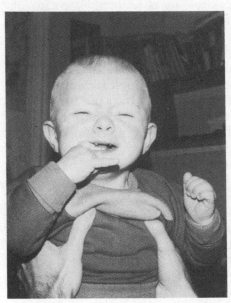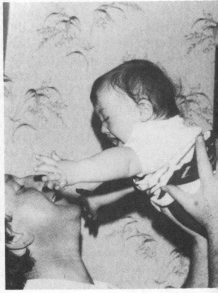

Two-way communication. Thus far, the baby's communications
have been in the eye of the beholder, usually his mother. But it
doesn't take long before a baby realises that he can control the
behaviour of his care-giving adults or of his brothers and
sisters. He discovers that he can get them to do things for him.
His messages are now deliberate and purposeful; *he knows
what he means.* How did this come about? It was mainly
through his mother's responsiveness to his *unintentional*
messages. You see, the sounds and gestures he made almost
instinctively were presumed by the mother to mean something.
The baby sent the message but the mother supplied the
meaning. As they became more attuned to each other through
daily practice, the child could start to see a connection—'if I do

this, mother does that.' He discovered the meaning his mother had given to his gestures. That is the beginning of intentional communication. Once the child and the mother both know the meaning, *intentional* communication can begin.

Summary
1 Communication begins at birth and continues throughout infancy with the child sending *unintentional* or unplanned messages to the mother or care-giver.
2 The mother *responds* to the child's message as if the baby were trying to express a specific meaning. She 'reads' his message as if it were intentional and responds appropriately.
3 The infant gradually learns that his *different* behaviours get different *responses* from his care-giver. He knows what he means when he does certain actions and expects a particular response from his parents. His messages are now *intentional* and more *specific*.
4 All this growth occurs long before the child starts to talk.

Activity 1a: Checklist—Early gestures and sounds
If you have a child who is not yet using clear words to indicate his or her needs, look at the list of *gestures* on the checklist.

* Tick any that you have observed your child using, or can recollect him using in the past.
* Note what *meaning* you think the child's gesture has. Your child may sometimes use the *same* gesture to mean different things. Put down all the meanings you can think of beside that gesture.
* Your child may also use some gestures that are not listed in the checklist. These gestures can be added at the bottom of the list.

Activity 1b: Early messages
You might like to try this activity instead of, or as well as the previous one.

* Look at the messages on the second checklist. These are ones which even quite young babies can send.
* Tick those which your child sends or which you can recollect him sending in the past.

CHECKLIST: EARLY GESTURES AND SOUNDS

Child's Name:..

Gesture and/or Sound	✓	Meaning(s)
Cries		
Coos and smiles		
Waves arms in the air		
Reaches with one or both arms		
Looks from adult to specific object and back		
Points		
Tugs at skirt, or arm		
Jumps up, down		
Turns head away		
Holds object out to you		
Bangs object		
Touches door		
Both arms held high		
Touches hand to mouth		
Other Gestures/Sounds Your Child Uses		

* Write down *how* he gets the message across. Try to picture it happening and write down as much detail as you can. For example, one father wrote against the item about *no more food*: 'Screwed up face, turned head from side-to-side and slid down in his chair.'

When you have done these two activities, you may be surprised at how much communicating your child is doing and at the many ways he uses to get his message across. But a stranger would probably not be able to work out his meanings. Hence, the most important people in developing a child's ability to communicate are those closest to him in his everyday life and activities.

HOW COMMUNICATION DEVELOPS

Obviously a child who is *active* will make *more* demands, send *more* messages and receive *more* responses from the care-giver. He has more opportunities to learn that communication works. As the infant grows and develops, he gains better control of his movements and sounds, his messages become more precise, and it is easier for his mother to interpret his messages and respond to him quickly. This in turn strengthens the child's *motivation* to communicate, encouraging him to further efforts. A ready response from his mother also reduces the *frustration* that occurs when the child's messages are not understood.

Frustration. A certain amount of frustration is inevitable when the child's messages are immature. With all the good will in the world, even the most responsive care-giver can fail to understand some of the messages that are sent using only gestures and crude sounds. A little frustration is not harmful to a child so long as most of his communicative attempts *are understood*. At a later stage frustration may even have a positive effect in motivating the child to make his messages more precise. This may occur when he begins to mix with people other than his immediate family—relatives, neighbours, other children, or perhaps at playgroup or pre-school, where the teacher and other children will not be familiar with his gestures

CHECKLIST: EARLY MESSAGES

Child's Name:..

Messages	Has your child sent these messages?	The way my child sends the message
I'm hungry, I want something to eat		
I'm lonely, I want some company		
I don't want any more—I don't like that food		
I need to 'poo'— go to the toilet		
Look at that over there! I want that		
Don't go away or put me down . . . stay with me		
Any other messages your child sends?		

and sounds, and he will experience more difficulty in making himself understood.

Physically handicapped children. Too much frustration, however, can make a child feel that there is little point in trying to send messages. Problems can arise with children who are physically handicapped. They are unable to use their bodies to make the early gestures used by normally developing children. The mothers of these children need to be even more alert than those of non-handicapped children to watch for signs that their child is trying to indicate his needs and communicate feelings. Sometimes an early indication may be a change of expression in the child's eyes, or in the direction of his gaze. The important thing is to prevent him feeling so frustrated in his attempts at communicating that he stops trying and remains passive, not making any demands at all.

Passive children. A second problem which requires particular care on the part of the mother is the case of the so-called 'sleepy' baby, who lies endlessly without crying, or smiling or making any other efforts to interact with those taking care of him. This can happen if a child is on medication for the control of epilepsy or other medical conditions. In situations such as these it is important to try and *draw out* responses from the child. This is one of the most effective methods we have of teaching children to do new things. For example, you need to exaggerate your greetings, keeping your face close to the child's. Raise his arms as you lift him up, help him to wave his arms and to point at all sorts of things that might interest him—coloured mobiles, tinkling bells, the moon through the window, or the dog eating his dinner. Tell him what you are doing as you change his nappy, bath him, dress him, get ready to go shopping or to visit grandma. Keep his favourite foods in sight but just out of reach, to try and encourage some indication of his 'wanting'.

Watch closely and encourage *any* signs of responsiveness— even an eye movement—and when they are few and far between, continue to *show* the child how we make demands and how we interact with toys and people and how we respond to these interactions. Your patience will usually be rewarded, first by responses which you had to work hard to get, later by some spontaneous responses and, finally, by seeing your child do things of his own accord.

Remember all children have to be able to send or *initiate* messages as well as being able to *respond* to other people. It is important that infants learn to master both roles in their exchanges with adults. We shall come back to this when we describe the different messages children send (p. 52).

Summary
1   Infants *need* a *responsive care-giver* to help develop:
    a)   their *motivation* to communicate;
    b)   their *skill* in *sending messages* and in *responding to* the people who matter most in their daily lives.
2   The *responsive* adult will:
    a)   watch closely for the child's messages;
    b)   respond promptly and appropriately;
    c)   encourage the child in his attempts to send increasingly varied messages;
    d)   help the child to make his messages clearer;
    e)   avoid frustration—try and work out what he is trying to tell you from what you know about his immediate activities and interests;
    f)   try to *elicit* responses from passive, unresponsive or physically handicapped children.

THE FORM OF EARLY COMMUNICATION

We have been talking about communication and the sending of 'messages' with children who are not yet able to talk. How does the child manage this difficult task and how is it that adults are able to 'understand' what the child is 'saying'?

The *child's* earliest messages are sent using:
    a)   sounds,
    b)   gestures, or
    c)   a combination of sounds and gestures, e.g. 'ug' with arms raised, as he strains to be lifted out of the cot, or 'ba-ba' as he points to his bottle sitting on the kitchen bench.

The *parent* understands the child's sounds and gestures because he or she is:

a) tuned in to the child's needs—*knows* when the child is hungry and what he likes to eat and that he has a bottle at bed-time;

b) familiar with the child's everyday world—the activities, objects and people within it—knows that he *always* wants his rubber duck in the bath with him and that teddy sleeps in the corner of his cot, behind his pillow.

Parents are very good at guessing because they know their child so well.

This is important for successful communication at *all* stages —even with adults—but it is vital when one partner is an immature communicator.

The use of gestures is not limited to young children. Adults use them a great deal in their everyday communication— pointing to indicate direction, wagging a finger—perhaps to emphasise a point they are making, or putting their head on one side to indicate surprise or perhaps disbelief. These gestures make our communication clearer to the person we are addressing, even if they are not essential to the understanding of the message. With young infants, they are the only way of getting their message across.

Stages. The way in which children communicate changes as the child matures. Five broad stages can be identified, but these overlap and you should not be surprised if your child is doing things from two or more stages.

1 *Global gesture and crying*—it could mean, 'I'm cold', 'I'm 'hungry', 'I want to be picked up and cuddled', 'I *don't* want my cereal this morning!'

The earliest messages consist of an all-purpose cry, frequently accompanied by global movement of the whole body, with arms thrashing, legs kicking and the body turning from side to side. Conversely, the earliest sounds of pleasure, cooing and gurgling, may be accompanied by similar but less violent random body movements.

2 *A more specific gesture accompanied by a sound*—for example, 'Ah, ah!' as the child stands up in his cot and

points at teddy on the floor; 'Wa-wa-wa' as the child bangs on the back door; 'Bwa' as the child tags at your trouser legs. As the baby grows, he begins to use a number of sounds and babbling noises, any of which may be accompanied by movements, such as pointing and reaching.

3   *Consistent sound, usually linked with a gesture*—e.g. 'Whee!' with throwing gesture as an invitation for you to play ball with him; 'brm-brm' as a car is pushed across the floor; 'dat' as child points to his shoes in response to your question, 'What do we put on next?' Here the child has reached a stage where he uses a *particular* sound (often linked to a specific gesture) for each type of message. He has made up his *own* words and never uses them except when he wants to refer to this specific object or activity— 'whee' will only be used for the act of *throwing* and 'brm-brm' is his word for car. He has now learnt that we have different sounds to refer to different objects and activities

and that we generally use the same word to refer to a specific object or action. But the child has not yet mastered the proper word. Those who know him well, soon learn *his* words and can respond appropriately. Indeed, the whole family may begin to use the child's word instead of the proper one.

The important thing to understand about these 'special' words is that they are often peculiar to each child; children develop their own 'words'—they are not taught—and the words may not be used by any other child, although a few words such as, 'brm-brm', 'quack-quack', 'miaow', 'ta', are used quite widely. These invented words are sometimes referred to as 'protowords' because they are *like* real words and are used instead of proper words.

4   *Single words, with or without gestures*—e.g. the child says, 'Hat', gives the hat to his mother and pats his head, indicating that he wants her to put it on him; or he bangs on the front door and says, 'Open'; or points to the biscuit tin and says, 'More'. As the child matures, his consistent sounds or 'protowords' will be exchanged for the proper word. He picks these up when his mother *says the real word* to him each time he uses his own word, even though she responds to what he was communicating as if he had been using the real word.

A child's first words are the names of important people or actions or objects in his everyday life—things he *wants* to talk about and to share with you. He may still accompany his single words with gestures, just to make sure you know what he wants—it's *that* tin that has his favourite biscuits and he wants 'more'.

5   *Two words together, with* or *without gestures*—e.g. 'hat on', 'open door', 'more biscuit', 'daddy gone', 'throw ball'. The messages that he could send with single words are soon expanded to two words, as he manages to combine his words, so that he can tell you more precisely what he wants—'more drink', 'drink orange', 'daddy drink'.

By this stage, the child's message is more readily understood, although it may not measure up to our standards of polite social behaviour. If children find *three* words too difficult, they leave out 'please' and 'thank you', but if you are patient and encourage your child to express the really important messages that he is bursting to share with you, he will soon 'hear' the extra words that you use and will say them as soon as he can.

He has come a long way.

A mixture of stages. We must stress that children do not move smoothly from one stage to the next. Rather, they will often continue with gestures and vocalisations, even though they have begun to use short sentences. Indeed, adults do this, too—we point and make sounds like 'uh-uh' in the middle of our conversations. So do not discourage your child's use of gestures once he begins to talk; rather encourage the use of words as well as gestures.

Summary
The five stages of early communications are:

1   Global gestures and crying which could mean, 'I'm cold' or I'm hungry or 'I want to be cuddled'. | Birth |

2   More specific gestures with sounds, e.g. waving his arms in the air and gurgling with pleasure at the sight of his mother, which means, 'I'm pleased to see you'.

3   Consistent sound linked with a specific gesture, e.g. pointing to his teddy bear on the floor and saying, 'Dat, dat'.

4   Single words, with or without gesture, e.g. holding out his cup to mother and saying 'drink'.

5   Two words together, with or without gesture, e.g. tugging at his sister's arm and saying 'kick ball'.

| usually between 2 and 3 years |

THE RANGE OF EARLY MESSAGES
When we are good at talking and can string lots of words togther easily, we are able to send a lot of different messages with just one sentence. Indeed, we even have ways of using

sentences which let the listener know what we mean, even though we did not express it in the most obvious way. Here are two examples:

1 'That's a tall tower you're making, but would you clear the blocks away now because daddy will be home soon and then we'll have dinner.'
2 'Ooh! It's cold with that window open!'

In the first sentence there are several messages: a *comment* on the 'tall tower', a *request* to clear the blocks away and *information* regarding daddy's movements and dinner. The second sentence, which sounds like a comment on the weather, may really be a request to close the window and should result in the listener doing just that, because he should pick up what was *meant* and not merely what was said. This is much the same as adults responding to the unclear messages of young children in terms of what the adults think the child means.

Adults and older children also have different ways of speaking in different situations—slang expressions may be acceptable amongst our close friends but more formal language is required at the dinner table with grand-parents present.

The young child who is just learning to communicate, can send only *one message at a time* and the message may not be very clear. It may require the close attention of a caring adult to work out what it is the child is trying to say. But even using gesture and sound only, there is a range of basic messages which children manage to send and the list extends as they become capable of taking part in more complicated interactions with the important people in their lives. Table 2.1 lists the main types of messages that young children learn to send and indicates whether these are mainly in *reponse* to a message from you or whether the child *initiates* the message (see p. 54).

Requests and demands—The earliest messages sent by the infant are *demands* or *requests* for basic needs such as food, warmth or comfort, and these are soon extended to demands for *attention* from the important people in the child's life, demands for the *objects* that he is becoming familiar with, and later on demands for *action*—to be lifted up out of his cot, or pushed on a swing.

TABLE 2.1

Message type	Child's role in the interaction
Early messages Requests/demands —objects —attention —action	Initiation only
Protests/refusals	Response only
Greetings—welcoming —parting	Initiation and/or Response
Commenting—indicates —describes	Initiation and/or Response
Later messages Commenting —gives information	Initiation and/or Response
Questions—Answers —Asks	Response only Initiation only
Word play/imitation/ practising	Not involved in communication with another person

Protests and refusals—Another early message is that of *protest* or *refusal*—the capacity to reject food or toys that are offered when they are *not* wanted, to protest when returned to the cot against his will, or left behind while his mother and father go out. Later examples include the assertion of independence that is evident when the child refuses to do things initially at home, and later in pre-school and school settings. It might be a refusal to wear his *red* shirt, or to stand in line at the playgroup before going outside to play.

Greetings—Greetings are learnt early, e.g. cooing and smiling at the sight of his mother's face. This early greeting develops later into more conventional verbal greetings, for welcoming and parting from people. Gestures can remain an important part of these behaviours, as they do in the 'waving' action that accompanies 'bye-bye'.

Commenting—Another more sophisticated and easily over-looked early message is *commenting*. Here the child attempts to 'talk' about the important things in his environment, and to share this information with others.

a) *Indicating.* The earliest form of this may take place in combination with the *demand for attention*, mentioned earlier, where a child will attract the mother's attention and transfer his gaze from her face to the object of his interest, perhaps combined with an early 'reaching' or 'pointing' gesture. This *indicating* behaviour develops as the child becomes more mobile and is engaged in exploring his environment. He frequently draws his mother's attention to objects with which he is actively engaged or which interest him—his teddy bear, or a particular sauce-pan that he likes to play with in the kitchen or a novel object such as a cuckoo clock.

b) *Describing.* This is closely related to 'describing' behaviour in which the child will not only '*indicate*' an object but also *comment* upon it, using gestures and sound before he has the *words* to tell you what interests him. He may sit banging a drum and say 'da! da! da!' as he looks at you, telling you as clearly as he can what he is doing! To understand these early descriptions and comments you will need to be involved with the child in his setting, aware of what he is doing, and what he is attending to.

c) *Giving information.* A much more difficult 'message' to send is one where the child is trying to tell you about an object or experience that you have not shared with him—telling you that he saw a bird peck a worm from the lawn while you were inside washing the dishes. *Giving information* of this sort, about events not occurring in the shared present, is much more difficult to send, and to understand, especially if the child has to rely only on gesture and sound to give you his message. This type of 'message' tends to develop a little later than the ones we have already mentioned.

Questions—Asking and *answering* questions is another complicated task that the child has to learn, and one that takes a little
longer than demands, protests, greetings and commenting.

a) *Answers.* Early answers are made using sound and gesture,
    perhaps a pointing or indicating response. Later the child
    may reply verbally, once the appropriate word or words
    have been learnt.

b) *Asks questions.* The asking of early questions may take the
    form of attracting attention to the relevant object or
    activity, accompanied by a questioning look and a
    questioning intonation with whatever sound is used.
    Later, questions may take the form of a single word or
    two, again used with questioning intonation. Proper
    'question sentences', with inverted word order, do not
    develop for some years. However, parents should not
    worry if their child does not use the correct sentence
    structure; it is more important that he should ask
    questions and that the information he seeks be supplied to
    him.

Word play, imitation and practising—Sometimes young children
will say a single sound over and over, as though they are
listening to themselves. Sometimes they imitate a sound or
word that they may have heard *you* make, and they will say it
repeatedly, without expecting a response from you, and
without attaching any *meaning* to their sounds. This usually
takes place in non-*communicative* situations, such as when the
child is lying in his cot or playing on his own. We mention it
here for the sake of completeness.

Importance of messages
The importance of these early messages, with the exception of
the 'word play', lies in the *purpose* they serve in the child's life,
increasing his capacity to make demands on and to effect
changes in his environment, to obtain information and to
interact satisfactorily with the important people around him.

A second important aspect concerns the practice they give
the child in taking the role of responding or initiating during an
interaction.

As Table 2.1 shows, with some messages the child sends, he

is *initiating* the interaction and the adult *responding*, and in other situations this position is reversed. *Requests* or *demands*, and *asking questions*, are examples where the child tends to initiate the exchange, whereas *protesting* or *refusing* and answering questions occur in *response* to adult initiations. *Greetings* and *commenting*—indicating, describing and giving information— can occur both as initiations and responses. It is important that the child should be able to play both roles in the exchange and, where this does not occur spontaneously, he can be helped by having the adult *elicit* the behaviour, or encourage it by showing him what to do. We mentioned this on p. 47 and we shall return to it when we deal with encouraging early communication (p. 72).

Summary

Table 2.2 gives you examples of each type of message. It also shows you how the form of the message changes as the child's communication develops from gestures to consistent sounds and to the use of two or more words.

As you read through the Table, try to recall things your children do that are similar.

TABLE 2.2: Summary of the types of messages children send

Child's Message	Early gesture with non-specific vocalisation	Consistent sound with or without gesture	Single word with or without gesture	Two words with or without gesture	Adult form of message
Requests/demands					
—objects	Reaching + sound	Reaching + 'ta'	'teddy' ± reaching	'want teddy'	'I want my teddy bear'
—action	Tugging + sound	Tugging + 'mum mum'	'Mummy' ± tugging	'Mummy come'	'Come and open the door for me'
—attention	Arms raised + cry	Arms raised + 'u'	'up' + arms raised	'Mummy up'	'Please lift me up, Mummy'
Protests/Refusals	Shakes head + sound	Shakes head + 'na!'	'No!' ± shakes head	'No hair!'	'I don't want you to dry my hair!'
Greetings					
—welcoming	Smiles + coos	Smiles + 'hwa'	'Hiya' + smile	'Hiya, Daddy'	'Hello, Daddy'
—parting	Waves + gurgles	Waves + 'ba'	'Bye' + wave	'Bye-bye, Mummy'	'Good-bye, Mummy'
Commenting					
—indicates	Context specific: Points + sound	Points + 'woof'	'Doggie' ± points	'That doggie'	'That's a dog'

TABLE 2.2: Summary of the types of message children send (Contd)

Child's Message	Early gesture with non-specific vocalisation	Consistent sound with or without gesture	Single word with or without gesture	Two words with or without gesture	Adult form of message
—describes	Cups hands + sound	Cups hands + 'ba'	'Ball' ± cups hands	'Big ball'	'It's a big ball'
—gives information about past events	Waves arms + sound	Waves arms + 'chuff'	'Train' ± waves arms	'Train gone'	'I saw the train go by'
Questions					
—answers	Points + sound	Points + 'oink'	'Pig' ± points	'Big pig!'	'I saw a big pig on TV'
—asks	Looks at adult + sound with question intonation	Looks at adult + 'da?' with question intonation	'Daddy?' + questioning look	'Daddy coming?'	'Is Daddy coming home soon?'
Word play/ imitation/ practising	waves arms + 'ba-ba-ba'	Hand in front of eyes + 'boo!'	Hand in front of eyes: 'Tommy'	'Where Tommy?' (repeated with/without variations)	(not applicable)

GET SET

YOUR CHILD'S COMMUNICATIONS

Whether or not your child is talking, he is probably well able to tell you things. In this part, we describe activities you can do that will prove this and provide you with forms on which you can note down what your child did. When you read back over them, you will be able to see your child's strengths and weaknesses when it comes to communicating.

If you do not want to write on the book, you can make a photocopy of the forms, or else draw them out on a sheet of paper.

If your child is not yet using clear words

We suggest you try activity 2a. This is designed to let you see the different *ways* in which your child communicates. It also lets you see how often he initiates and responds to messages.

If your child has started to talk

Activity 2b is more suitable for you. Here you will discover the types of messages your child sends and it also lets you see how often your child initiates or responds to messages.

YOU CAN DO BOTH ACTIVITIES IF YOU WISH: ACTIVITY A IS GOOD PRACTICE FOR ACTIVITY B.

Activity 2a: Early messages

On pages 62 and 63 you will find two forms—one entitled '*Children's Responses*', the other, '*Child's Initiations*' (i.e. done by self).

The idea is that you watch your child carefully for a day, as you go about your usual tasks with him—dressing, meal-times, washing, playing, bath-time, etc. You note on the form the 'messages' you picked up from your child. We have given you three examples on each form—you might like to read them now.

* Form 1 is for recording your child's responses to what you said or did.
* Form 2 is for recording the messages your child initiated, i.e. those he sent to you.
* If your child is active, you will have many more messages

than there is room for on the forms. You might need to continue your records on other sheets of paper. However, you *do not* need to note every message. Rather try to record:

    a) examples of the *different* ways in which your child communicates;

    b) communications that surprised you; ones you did not expect or had noticed for the first time.

* The examples given on the forms show you what you might write down.

* Decide *when* you will observe—pick a day that is typical and one when you are not likely to be too busy.

Good luck.

The completed forms
What do the forms tell you about your child's communications? These questions might help you:

Form 1. How successful were you in getting responses from your child?
Even very young or severely handicapped children are quite good at picking up their parent's messages. If your child is not particularly responsive there are ways of encouraging him (see p. 47).

Comparing Forms 1 and 2, does your child have more responses than initiations, or are they roughly the same?
The more inactive your child is, the more likely you are to have more responses than initiations. But as children become more active, their initiations start to become more frequent and varied. We shall describe ways of encouraging your child to initiate messages on p. 72.

How does your child communicate? Is he using only gestures; gestures and noises; consistent sounds with actions; maybe even words?
Recall the five stages we described earlier (p. 52). Which one would you say best describes your child? You now have some idea of the developments you can expect in the future. For example, if most of your child's communications consist of gestures and/or noises, then you could expect him to start using some consistent sounds, linked with more specific gestures. Indeed, you may even have noted a few instances of this already.

62

ACTIVITY 2a. FORM 1: CHILD'S RESPONSES		
What did you say and do—words + gesture?	What did the child do in response?	What was the context in which the interaction took place?
Examples a 'Hello' + arms extended towards child lying in the cot	Child shifted gaze and looked at my face	Getting up in the morning
b 'Do you want a biscuit'? + holding biscuit out towards child	Reached to take the biscuit	Morning tea time
c 'Quack-quack'— playing with rubber duck in the bath	Child reached for duck and laughed	Bath-time
1		
2		
3		
4		
5		
6		
7		
8		

CONTINUE ON ANOTHER SHEET OF PAPER

ACTIVITY 2a. FORM 2: CHILD'S INITIATIONS

	What did the child do? Note gesture and sound	What do you think the child was trying to say?	What did you do in response?	What was the *context* in which the interaction took place?
a	*Examples* 'Ah, ah, ah!' jumping up and down holding on to the edge of the cot	'I want to be taken out of here!'	Lifted child out of cot	Early morning after night's sleep
b	'Uh, uh!' and turning head aside and pushing my hand away	'I don't *want* scrambled egg this morning!'	Tried again and then gave the child a piece of toast	Breakfast time
c	'Ooh' and pointing	'look at that'	Said, 'it's a fire engine'	Walking down the street to the shop
1				
2				
3				
4				
5				
6				
7				

CONTINUE ON ANOTHER SHEET OF PAPER

How much variety is there in the messages your child sent?
Do you remember the different types of messages described on
Table 2.2 (page 58)? On form 1, have you any examples of
your child *protesting/refusing*, responding to your *greeting*, or
comment, or *answering* your question? Likewise, on Form 2,
are there *requests/demands* from your child, *greetings*,
comments or *questions asked*? If you have no examples of some
particular type of communication—and that's quite likely—this
is something you might encourage your child to do (see p. 72).

*Are there times/situations when your child is more likely to
communicate?*
You may be able to spot a pattern emerging as you read down
the columns headed '*context*'. Are these the times when you
and the child are involved in the same activity—like feeding,
bathing, etc? On the other hand, children can communicate in
all sorts of different contexts and your forms may show this
happening.

We hope you now have a better idea of what communication is
all about. You may be surprised at how much communication
takes place between you and your child. Many parents take this
for granted and are inclined to think that their child is worse
then he actually is. You should also have some clues as to how
you might encourage your child to communicate more. Pages
72 to 80 will give you more details.

Activity 2b: Messages
This activity is recommended for active children who have
started to talk.

Table 2.2 described the range of messages that children can
send (p. 58) This activity will let you see just which messages
your child is sending; how he is sending them and in what
situations. Even when a child *can* use words, you may find that
he will still send some messages by using gestures only.

We suggest you pick two or three times (around five to ten
minutes long) during the day when you can keep a record of
your child's messages.

Remember:
a)   Some types of messages will occur only in particular

situations—greetings are most likely early in the morning, or when someone is going to work or coming home, or if you have visitors.

b) Despite this, choose times that suit you, when you are doing the ordinary things that you do with the child every day. These may include meal-times, washing-up, playing indoors or out in the garden, bath-time, story-time, watching television, bed-time.

c) It is best to choose a time when you do not want the child to do anything in particular, but be prepared to be responsive, no matter what he is doing.

Note down on Form 3 all the messages you picked up from the child in that session:

a) write down what the child said or did;

b) what sort of 'message' you think it was (refer to Table 2.2);

c) the situation or *context* in which it occurred;

d) whether it was *initiated* (I) by the child, or a *spontaneous response* (S) to something you said or did, or whether it was an *elicited response* or *imitation* of something *you* said. (E).

For example, if you were dressing the child after his bath and you said, 'What do we put on next?' and your child did not reply, you might say, 'Shoes! we put on shoes next. What do we put on next?' This time the child says, 'Shoes!' —and you would mark this as an 'Answers questions' (E) to indicate that the child managed to answer your question, but only after you had given him a little help, by telling him what the answer was and then asking him again. We call this *prompting*. It helps the child work out what it is that he should say, allows him to *hear* the word and gives him another chance to say it himself.

The examples that have been filled out on Form 3 will give you an idea of how to make your own record. Have a look at it now, then decide when you will observe your child..

Summary

Once you have collected enough examples of your child's communications from a variety of different situations, you can

ACTIVITY 2b. FORM 3: CHILD'S MESSAGES (Example)

Child's Name: Jamie   Date.....................

What did the child say or do?	What was happening?	Initiation (I) Spontaneous response (S) Elicited response or imitation (E)	'Message type'
rattles cot rails	standing up in cot in the morning	I	Demand —action
points to mirror and says 'Dat!'	carrying him down-stairs—mother: 'Where's Jamie?'	SR	Question —answers
'Ahh' + shakes head	Pushes cereal away at breakfast	SR	Refusal
'Mmm + pushes cup to mother	Breakfast—finishes milk + wants more	I	Demand —object
'Woof?' + looks at mother, points to the door	Questioning look at mother with dog scratching at door	I	Question —asks
'Brm' + pushes car	Playing with car on carpet	I	Comment —describing
'Yiyi' + jumps up and down	Daddy walked into room	I	Greeting —welcomes
'Oo'	Child puts spoon in drawer and imitates mother, 'That's a spoon'	E	Commenting —describing
'Wawawawa'	Child chanting sound in his cot, over and over	Non-communicative sounds	Word play

ACTIVITY 2b. FORM 4: SUMMARY OF CHILD'S MESSAGES (Example)

Child's Name: Jamie   Date:.....................

Message type	Gesture and/or sound				One or two words			
	I	SR	E	Total	I	SR	E	Total
Requests/demands				2				
—objects	1			1				
—attention								
—action	1			1				
Protests/refusals		1		1				
Greetings				1				
—welcoming	1			1				
—parting								
Commenting				2				
—indicates								
—describes	1		1	2				
—gives information								
Questions				2				
—answers		1		1				
—asks	1			1				
Word play/imitation/ practising		1		1				
Total	5	2	1	8				

I = Initiation
SR = Spontaneous Response
E = Elicited response or imitation

summarise them on Form 4. This will give you a clear picture of the different types of messages he is using, how he sends them (is he using a mixture of gesture and words?) and whether they are initiations or responses.

On the Example Form 4, Jamie's messages have been summarised. Here's what we did:

On Form 3, the first communicative message recorded was 'rattling cot rails'. This was a *demand for action* which Jamie *initiated* (I). Hence, on Form 4 we placed a tick in the row labelled *Requests/Demands–action* and in the column under Gesture and/or Sound for I.

His second message was an *answer to a question*—a spontaneous response, again conveyed by gesture and sound. The tick went in the second row from the bottom under SR—gesture and/or sound.

And so we continued, until all the messages had been recorded in the summary form. We then totalled the rows and columns, as shown on the form.

You should now complete a summary form for your child.

What the form tells you
If you look at the summary of Jamie's messages you will notice that he is not using all the message types listed. He did not make any demands for attention, and we have no examples of a greeting when someone is going away. He did not 'indicate' or 'give information'. You will have noticed that all Jamie's messages were sent using gesture and sound. He is not yet using many 'real' words but he is using some consistent sounds and proto-words such as 'woof' and 'brm' to mean 'dog' and 'car', so it will probably not be long before he does start to use real words.

We would not really expect Jamie to be able to 'give information' about something he has not shared with his mother when he is still using gesture to get his message across, but his parents might look out for instances of him making demands for attention, using greetings to say 'good-bye' as well as 'hello', and indicating things that he is playing with or interested in. If he does not, they might try and give him plenty of opportunities to do these things, perhaps modelling them

ACTIVITY 2b. FORM 3: CHILD'S MESSAGES

Child's Name:................. Date:....................

What did the child say or do?	What was happening	Initiation (I) Spontaneous response (S) Elicited response or imitation (E)	'Message type'

CONTINUE ON ANOTHER SHEET OF PAPER

ACTIVITY 2b. FORM 4: SUMMARY OF CHILD'S MESSAGES

Child's Name:................. Date:....................

Message type	Gesture and/or sound				One or two words			
	I	SR	E	Total	I	SR	E	Total
Requests/demands								
—objects								
—attention								
—action								
Protests/refusals								
Greetings								
—welcoming								
—parting								
Commenting								
—indicates								
—describes								
—gives information								
Questions								
—answers								
—asks								
Word play/imitation/ practising								
Total								

I = Initiation
SR = Spontaneous Response
E = Elicited response or imitation

for him, as his mother did when he imitated 'spoon' after she had said it for him.

It is useful to know that Jamie is willing to try to imitate things his mother does and says because this is an easy way of showing him how to do things he has not yet learnt. It is good, too, that he was initiating in a variety of situations, and he responded spontaneously to his mother's question and to the offer of food.

This summary of Jamie was compiled from a very small sample of messages. You would want to collect many more examples of your child's messages before you felt you had a full picture of what he is able to do. That is why we suggested you observed your child on two or three occasions. Keep the sheets handy over the next couple of days and note down 'new' messages he sends or ones at other times of the day.

This will give you a much more comprehensive picture of his skill at communicating than you will get from choosing just two or three situations in one day. It will ensure that he has had the *opportunity* to use all the different types of messages—and if his summary sheet indicates one or two message types that he *is not* using, you will be fairly sure that it is because he does not know *how* to, and not because he did not have a chance to show it. So look at *your* child's summary sheet and see what sort of picture you are getting about his skill in sending early messages, and his responses to those that you send to him.

* *How does your child communicate?*
  Is he using mostly gestures and/or sound or mostly words and/or sentences?
* *What are the messages he sends most often?*
* *Are there any messages he does not send?*
* *Does your child have more initiations than responses, or are they roughly the same?*
* *Are you able to elicit responses from your child? Does he try to imitate you?*

Armed with this information, you will know what to look out for as you read about ways of encouraging children's early messages.

GO

ENCOURAGING COMMUNICATION
Your goals are:

1 To increase the *range* of messages your child sends.
2 To ensure that your child is both *initiating* and *responding*.
3 To ensure that your child's messages become increasingly clear over time—that there is a progression from relying mostly on gesture to using words.

Learning to send a wide range of messages, to express their needs, to ask questions, or to refuse things that they do not want is a very hard task for some small children. They need a lot of help from caring adults and siblings to help them learn to do this. We cannot 'teach' it in the same way that we teach reading or writing.

Encouraging initiations
You need to use all the everyday situations where you are

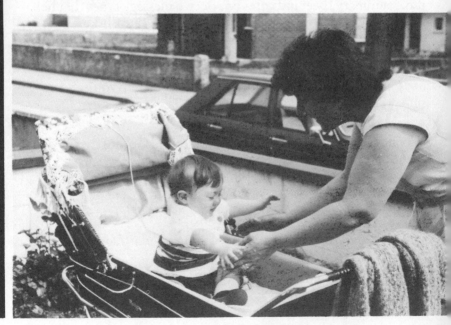

involved in joint activities with your child—and look for opportunities to *encourage* him to make demands and to show you things that interest him. For example, when you go into his room in the morning, give him time to greet you and to indicate that he wants to be lifted out of his cot. Hold out your arms towards him—but not quite within reach—and he may then lift his arms to *tell* you that he wants to be picked up. When you are dressing him, ask him which piece of clothing we put on next, whether he wants his blue or his red shirt. You can accidentally drop something and see if he will draw your attention to it, or even pick it up. At meal-times, *ask* him if he wants toast or egg, milk or juice. Let him help you lay the table, or put things away in the kitchen, and say the names of the things you are handling—spoon, cup, plate, etc. Leave his special mug off the table and see if he will protest if you give him a drink in another one, or whether he will 'demand' it. When you are playing with him and his toys, comment simply on what you are doing—'wash teddy'—or point to the different farmyard animals as they go into the field and say, 'Which one next?' or, 'What's that?' when you look at a picture book.

Encouraging more advanced forms of communication

In ways like these you can provide plenty of opportunities for different sorts of messages. You can 'show' him how to send those he is not very good at yet. You need to *accept* his responses, no matter how limited, and respond quickly to any attempt he makes at initiating. If you watch carefully you can usually work out what he means, even if the sounds are unclear and the gesture not very specific. Only insist on a *more* specific response if you *know* that he can make one. So accept his *pointing* to the biscuit jar as a *request* for a biscuit, and do not expect him to *say* 'biscuit' or 'biscuit, please' unless you know that he can say it. If he stands and cries when he wants a biscuit, and the biscuit jar is out of reach, show him how to point to the jar—and give him a biscuit as soon as he makes any attempt. You can *say* the word 'biscuit' as he does this, and gradually he will learn to use it, too; once he can, you will no longer accept his pointing gesture only. In this way, by accepting and encouraging the child's earliest form of his message, you can help him move from gesture only, to gesture combined with a sound, then a single word, two words together, and finally a complete sentence.

For example:

1 Stretches/reaches up to biscuit jar.
2 Points to jar and looks at mother, then back at jar.
3 Points and says, 'eh-eh' (non-specific vocalisation).
4 Points and says, 'Bikky.'
5 Points and says, 'Want biscuit.'
6 'Want biscuit, please.'
7 'Please may I have a biscuit?'

Needless to say, this will take two or three years with most children. Remember, too, that the first step is often the most vital. If you had refused to respond to his early gesture or ignored it, he would have become frustrated and angry. The opportunity for a satisfactory communicative exchange would have been missed and the learning chain would not have got underway. So look for situations that are causing the child frustration and provide him with a gesture or word to use, whichever is appropriate for his stage, and then respond to it very quickly when he does use it. If he is slow to pick it up then model it for him. An example of this may be when the child wants to go outside but cannot open the door. Frustration frequently leads to crying, so show the child how to tap the door with his hand, and as soon as he does this open it for him. Then, as he taps the door, say 'Open!' You will have started a chain of learning that in time will lead your child to say 'Open', then 'Open door' and later, 'Open door, please, Mummy!'

Encouraging specific 'messages'

Requests/demands—Sometimes we are so quick to anticipate our children's needs that we do not allow them the opportunity to make demands on us. Other brothers and sisters can be guilty of this, too, and need to have it explained to them that the baby needs a chance to try and do things for himself. A child who has not learnt to express his needs and make demands at home, may have a very difficult time when he enters pre-school. There is perhaps a particular tendency to be

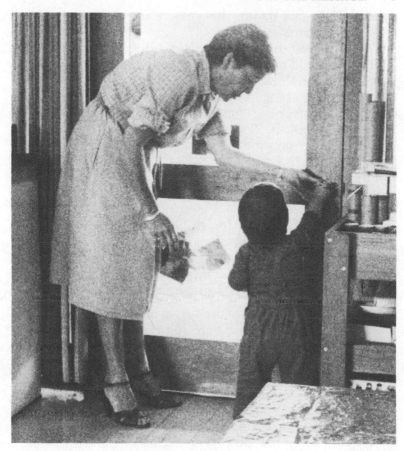

over-protective when a child is handicapped, either physically or mentally.

To encourage children to make requests or demands, it is necessary to watch closely to see what objects and activities are important to them. It is then possible to make it difficult for the child to reach the toy he wants, or his favourite story book, or his floating duck at bath-time. He will be forced to make a gesture or sound to indicate that he wants them. If he cries, you model the gesture, e.g. by pointing, or by saying 'want' or 'teddy' or 'quack-quack', or whatever you consider to be appropriate. If you persist for a few days, you may find that your child begins to use this gesture in other situations to indicate his wants.

You also need to develop the range of gestures and sounds which your child uses to attract your attention or to indicate that he wants to show you something. For instance, a child may tug at your clothing. Depending on his present stage, you could 1) encourage the child to put his hand in yours and lead you to his problem, 2) teach him a beckoning gesture, or 3) combine his action with the words 'look' or 'come' or similar sounds.

The important point is to be quick to respond to his earliest indication and to show him the new gesture, sound or word you want him to use.

Remember, it is good for children to tell you what they want. It is not a question of spoiling them or of giving in to them, or of them becoming anti-social. Your first priority is to ensure your child *wants* to communicate. Later you can teach him socially acceptable ways of communicating.

Protests/refusals—Most children have no difficulty learning to send this message, but there are some who remain passive in situations where they should 'protest'. For instance, a young child in a pre-school may need to be able to defend his possessions and his activities. There are several ways that we can encourage children to reject or refuse, if we watch them carefully at home. You can offer your child something that you *know* he does not like to eat or drink, or you could try stopping an activity you know he enjoys—being in the bath or on a swing, etc. If he does not respond clearly, you can encourage a response: model the word 'no' or a shake of the head or a gesture of pushing the object away. With practice, your child should catch on to the idea. You can then work on making his gestures clearer.

Further practice can come from an older brother or sister interfering in his game, upsetting his blocks, or taking his cars. Indeed, an older child can help provide many learning opportunities, both planned and unplanned. Be sure to explain *why* you are doing these slightly unkind things!

Greetings—There are many opportunities for greetings and farewells in the course of a normal day, with the comings and goings of the family to work or school. Then there are visitors to the house, shopping and outings, visiting friends or grand-parents, etc. Make sure that everyone involved with the child uses the same form of greeting, e.g. accompany the wave with 'hello' or 'bye'. Do not force the child to participate but always include him. In time he will start to join in.

Commenting (shared information)—If a child does not *indicate* things that interest him, you can model this behaviour when you are looking at a book or playing with toys. Point to a picture or object and suggest that he does the same. Make the game fun and encourage any attempt the child makes to show you something by responding very quickly. Point things out to him, and talk simply about what you are doing together when you are dressing him, at bath-times, in the kitchen, or walking in the park. If you encourage his early tentative gestures, it will probably not be long before he uses sounds, then words to tell you about things that are important to him, or that he has done.

Answers questions—Some children find this a very difficult task. It may be due to their reluctance to answer, or it may be because they do not fully understand what is expected of them.

It is important to keep your early questions very simple; make sure that the meaning is obvious to the child and then he can respond to what you are asking. 'What would you like to drink?' is much more difficult to answer than, 'Do you want milk or juice?'—and even this can be made more obvious if you have both juice and milk in front of you when you ask the question. You can present the child with choices in many situations—with food, toys, clothing.

If the child does not reply when you ask him to show you something in a book or whether he wants to go outside, then model the reply for him and give him time to respond (imitate you). But do not get into a confrontation. Move on to the next picture or open the door for him. If you keep giving him examples, he should pick up the idea and start answering for himself.

Beware, however, of bombarding your child with 'useless' questions—those to which you already know the answer. These put children on the spot; it is like an examination for them and they could quickly develop a dislike of answering questions—any question. Try to make your questions as genuine as possible, that is, you really want to know the answer.

Asks questions—This, perhaps, is the hardest 'message' of all, and it may be some years before a child can do it perfectly, especially with the difficult word order that we use for questions in English! But once again, you should think of situations that make it easier for him to ask a question. Begin by accepting a questioning look or intonation without demanding the complete question. 'Want?' accompanied by the gesture of holding a box of sweets towards you is also quite sufficient in the early stages and if 'want' is too difficult, 'uh?' and the gesture will do! This sort of behaviour can be modelled readily by brothers and sisters. Also, you can encourage the child to ask or find out 'who wants tea . . . toast, etc?'

Turn-taking games of all sorts can be used to encourage questions—picture lotto, where the question 'Who has the fox?' can be reduced to 'This one?' or even just the holding up of the card and looking questioningly at the other participants. Questions beginning with 'where?' and 'what?' can be taught by playing hiding games, where objects are hidden under different containers or around the room and turns taken by the child and parent at 'hiding' and 'asking'. Likewise, objects can be taken out of a 'surprise bag' and held up with the question, 'What's this?' It may not be long before your child has reached the stage where he seems to do *nothing* but ask you questions—and you may wonder why you worked so hard to teach him to do this!

Summary

These are some of the things that you can do to encourage children to use a range of messages. In all of them we advise you to show the child what to do and to build upon his efforts.

With handicapped children, you need to be very alert and to use the opportunities that arise in the course of their everyday lives, from getting up in the morning to going to bed at night—the first and last greetings of the day; while in between come requests and demands, refusals and protests, sharing of information and the asking and answering of questions.

Children need to practise with the people they know best

and in the relatively safe environment of the home before they start communicating with strangers in unfamiliar settings. This is just one of the many reasons why we keep saying that parents are in the best position to help their child.

The important points you have to remember are:

1 We communicate to get a *response* from other people—or because they want to get a *response* from us. We need a *reason* to communicate. Look for 'messages' that the child *needs* to be able to use to reduce his frustrations in his everyday life, such as ways of saying 'want', 'come', and 'do this for me, please'.

2 Look for situations where the child really *wants* something badly. These are ones where he will learn quickly that using the gesture or word you have shown him will get results faster than crying or throwing a tantrum.

3 Be quick to respond to what your child *says* and *does*. Copying what he does or says can be a good way of encouraging him to carry on and will give you more time to think about what he means if you are having problems understanding.

4 *Wait* for your child's response. Be sure that you give him enough time to respond—it could take as many as 30 seconds. Sometimes we are so impatient that if the child does not respond immediately we move on and say something else—and then that particular opportunity is lost.

5 Accept whatever response the child is capable of using. If he *cannot* use words, accept a gesture. If he *can* use words, let him know that you will do what he wants as soon as he uses the appropriate word. In this way you can help him move from immature to more mature ways of sending his messages.

6 Let *everybody* in the family know what you are expecting of the child so that they can react consistently to his demands, and expect the same things from him. If he is at pre-school, be sure that his teacher knows, too.

7 Use *every* opportunity that arises during the day to *encourage* him in his attempts to communicate with you—make it fun and rewarding for him so that he will *want* to continue and learn to do it better.

8   Your child is probably communicating more than you realise. His reponses may take an unexpected form, and you may need the skills of a detective to work out what he is trying to tell you. We know of a small boy who became very upset because his mother did not instantly understand that when he said 'boat' and pointed to the fridge, what he really wanted was an ice-cube! He had learnt the word 'boats' on their recent summer holiday, but his mother had failed to notice that the little plastic containers in which she had frozen the fruit juices were shaped like a boat.

It is from these experiences and others like them that children learn to communicate. They are the ideal basis for learning to talk, since the child starts to say words because *he* wants to. You do not have to teach him. A little help at the right time, in the right place and from a right-responsive parent is all that is needed.

SECTION THREE: NOW I UNDERSTAND

At birth children know nothing of the world outside the womb. Everything is new to them. They do not know for sure who is their mother and who is their father. Everyone is a stranger and probably, to them, all look alike; a reaction similar to that of Western travellers in China.

Likewise, every object is a novelty to them. They have no idea what each one is made of or what it is for.

Generally babies are fast learners. They use all their senses to gather information about the people and the objects that fill their waking hours. Understanding gradually dawns. Adults can easily take this learning for granted. They mastered it when they were babies but have no recollection of ever doing it. They have forgotten what a major task the baby is undertaking.

Yet children must learn the differences between people so that they can send appropriate messages to them and they must understand something about objects before they can 'ask' for them or use them appropriately or play with them 'properly'. As *understanding* grows, so, too, does the child's ability to communicate and his readiness to learn language. That is why we want you to know more about children's understanding.

What you will read about in this section

ON YOUR MARKS

What is understanding? We explain how children's knowledge of people and objects grows out of their everyday *experiences*; their capacity to *remember* what they discover with their senses and their ability to *recognise* people and objects by matching present experiences to their memories. It is only when they have this understanding that they can begin to learn a language.

The phases of understanding. We describe four phases in the growth of children's understanding about objects. These we call *exploring*, *relations*, *pretending* and *sequences*. We shall show you how these link with learning language.

GET SET

Assessing your child's understanding of objects. From observing your child playing with toys or common objects, you will be able to gauge his present level of understanding. From here you can go on to pick activities that further his understanding.

GO

Developing children's understanding. We show you ways of furthering your child's understanding through play and daily experiences. Here we must be honest and say that even with your best efforts, much will depend on your child. Understanding builds up inside a child's mind. You cannot control his senses, his memories or his thoughts. Moreover, handicaps of a child's senses (such as partial sight or hearing) or disability of body or brain, must hinder the development of understanding. Hence, there will be times when you will be disheartened at your child's rate of progress and frustrated that you cannot do more to help. Our advice is to take it a day at a time, doing what you can but realising that some children need more time than others for the learning to take place. Your biggest contribution is believing that someday it will happen.

ON YOUR MARKS

WHAT IS UNDERSTANDING?

Let us begin with something straightforward but rather crucial. How do you suppose babies learn to pick out their mothers from other people they come across? Think about it for a moment and see how your answers compare with ours.

* First, they need lots of *experience* of their mother's company and probably some experience of people other than their mother. We say 'probably' because all babies get this experience and hence it is impossible to decide how necessary it is for them to learn who is their mum.
* Second, they must, in some way, *remember* what is special about their mum—her looks, her voice, her smell, her touch or the way she holds them. We can surely say it is some, if not all of these things that babies remember.
* Third, the child has to *recognise* his mother. This means matching his memory with the present experience of the person. If they match, then it's mum! Of course, infants can be easily fooled. If mum wears a strange hat or talks in a different voice, the baby may dissolve into tears, convinced his mother has forsaken him.

In sum, then, a baby's knowledge of his mother grows through:

* *experiences*—which are frequent and personal;
* *remembering*—this may involve many senses—vision, hearing, smell, touch and movement;
* *recognising*—that is matching present experiences to past recollections.

It is not surprising, therefore that children get to know their mothers and fathers first. These are the people with whom they have most contact. But babies learn about other people in exactly the same way. And remember, they *know* the people long before they can ever put a name to them. Actions and gestures can easily say 'I know you'. Equally, if a child does not recognise his grandmother, say, then it will be very hard for him to learn her name, no matter how easy you make it—grandma, granny or nana. Recognition must come first.

Understanding objects

All that we have said about recognising people is just as true when it comes to learning about objects. A child's world—confined though it is—is still filled with lots of different objects. Nor do we mean playthings like rattles or dummy tits, but things like prams, cots, baths, bouncing cradles, clothes, towels, water, tins of talc, spoons and dishes. The list could go on and on. Every baby has to get to know these common objects. They are not born with this knowledge. They have to acquire it. They seem to do this in much the same way as they come to understand people. For instance, infants do not know the difference between a brush and cup. Nine-month-old babies will use these objects in exactly the same way—putting them to their mouth, turning them over, rubbing them against their face or hair, dropping or throwing them and so on. But out of this experience, and others, they gradually begin to recognise the differences, and then they will put the brush straight to their hair and the cup to their lips. They identify an object with an appropriate action. The babies achieve this understanding through their *experiences* of the objects, by *remembering* their essential features and by successfully *recognising* each. Later, they will come to call one a 'brush' and the other a 'cup'. Note, it is only when they understand the difference and show it in their actions that they learn that each has a different name. Understanding must come first. Children who merely repeat names without knowing what they are talking about, are speaking little better than parrots.

The first twelve months of an infant's life is a period of hidden learning as regards language. It is during this time—or even longer in the case of handicapped children—that he comes to understand the people and objects in his life. We shall have more to say about how children come to understand people and how they learn to get on with them in Section Four of the book, but now we shall take a closer look at how children's understanding of objects grows.

THE PHASES OF UNDERSTANDING

In recent years, we have learnt a great deal about the phases in children's development of understanding of objects and we can make more intelligent guesses as to how they acquire this knowledge, even if we do not know everything about it.

We shall begin by describing the phases in the growth of understanding.

Phase 1 Exploring

In this first phase, the child needs to experience the object at first hand. Two features are striking: first, the child is able to focus on only one object at a time; second, he performs the same actions with all sorts of different objects.

The major actions you can expect to see are given below; listed in the approximate order in which infants start to perform them.

1 *Mouthing*—the child grasps the object and brings it to his mouth; he may lick, mouth or chew it.
2 *Shakes/hits*—the child holds the object and shakes it or later may bang it against a surface (or another object), or, if the object is lying on the floor, he may hit it with his hand.
3 *Examines*—the child inspects the object by turning it round in his hand and looking at it carefully.
4 *Dropping/throwing*—these are deliberate movements, during which the child observes the object all the time—watching it fall or looking where it has landed.
5 *Feeling/rubbing*—the child rubs the object against his hand, face, etc., or rubs it against surfaces, such as table tops or the floor.

By the time the child can perform all these actions—and some require a great deal of motor control—he is well equipped to discover the physical properties of objects. For instance, he will know whether an object is hard or soft, whether it makes a noise or not, if it is solid or variable in shape, and so forth. This knowledge is crucial when it comes to telling the difference between objects. Incidentally, these exploratory actions, once acquired, stay with us for life. If I were to present you with a strange object—say an antique tool—very likely you would do some of the above actions in order to increase your *understanding* of it.

Objects always exist—During the exploring phase, infants learn something else about objects—namely that they continue to

exist even though the baby can no longer see or feel them. Adults may find it hard to believe that babies could ever think of objects 'disappearing', yet when you know little or nothing, it is not all that far-fetched. And if you observe babies closely, it certainly explains some of the odd things they do.

* If a favourite toy drops while they are exploring it, they make no attempt to search for it. They may just cry instead.

* If you take a toy from them and hide it under a cloth or box in full view of them, again they will not attempt to get it. They seem to believe it has gone—forever. However, if you leave part uncovered, then they will reach to get it. Through time, babies will start to look around for dropped objects or remove covers to fetch the toy they want. But another curious behaviour may then occur.

* You play a hiding game in which the child sees you hide a favourite toy under a cloth and each time he fetches it with

no difficulty. Then, for a change, you hide it under another object—a box, say—and guess what happens: the child only looks under the cloth, even though he has seen you hide it under the box.

It is as though young babies think that objects reappear when you perform a 'magical' action—in this case, reaching out for the cloth.

With more experience of exploring and playing with objects, they come to realise that objects are always around—it is merely a case of finding them. A quick test that they have begun to master this idea is as follows:

* Hide a favourite small toy or object under one cover—can the child get it? Then hide it under a different cover—does he get it this time? Now for the important part—cover the toy with your fist and pretend to leave it under the first cover but then place it under the second. If your child checks the first cover and goes on to look under the second, then he seems to know objects exist even though he can no longer see or feel them.

Psychologists and teachers describe this stage as the child understanding *object permanence*. There is a lot of evidence that children have to achieve this before they go on to learn the names of objects.

Phase 2 Relations

This phase grows out of the first. Here the child is concerned to find out how objects *relate* to one another; what you can do with them. The main feature of this stage is that the child can cope with two or more objects. At the simplest level, he may hold one in each hand and bang them together, or examine one, then another or throw them down simultaneously. He may empty objects out of a container or pull out one at a time. However, these 'crude actions' develop into more sophisticated movements—at least in terms of the child's understanding. He may put objects *inside* or on *top* of another. He may try to pull objects apart (lid off a box) or uncover them (remove a cloth to get at a rattle). Later he may try to put objects together (beads on to threader) or to use one object to get another (use a stick to get an object out of reach). All these developments are dependent on how well the child can control his hand and arm movements.

But that is not the whole story. Also important is the child's *understanding* of objects because this knowledge will guide and refine his movements. For instance, he has to *understand* that some objects will not fit inside others and that, no matter how good his hand control, he will never bring it about. Or another example we observed with infants playing with a ring-stacking toy, was their attempt to put a ring on to the stack by placing a ring ever so carefully at the bottom of the stick. This required a great deal of hand control, arguably more than was needed to raise the ring to the top of the stack and let it down on the stack. However, the children did not *understand* that the rings must be put on from the top. Instead they spotted that the rings ended up at the bottom and that is where they tried to put them on.

During this phase, children are not just developing further their understanding of objects, the new things they learn are:

* The actions that can be used in relating objects—putting in . . . on . . . or taking off . . . out. It is only when children are well practised at doing these actions that we could expect them to understand the words we use to describe them—'on' 'in', 'off'—and to realise that different actions have different words.

* A second thing they master has been termed an understanding of 'means-end' relationships. For instance, the child wants an object that is out of reach. He may stretch and stretch, cry in frustration or simply walk away. But a child who understands 'means-end' relationships can work out a plan—such as fetching a chair and using it to reach the object on the shelf; pulling on the tablecloth so that the object comes nearer; getting a stick and using it to retrieve the object from under the settee. In all these instances, the child manages to keep his goal or end result in mind while he finds a *means* of achieving it. Previously the infant wanted the object so much, he could not take his mind off it.

Some people have argued that language is another type of means to an end. The thirsty child has to think of the word 'drink' and then speak it while momentarily ignoring his desire to do something about getting a drink.

All children seem to master such forward-planning before they begin to use words meaningfully.

Phase 3 Pretend

This phase heralds a new era in children's understanding of objects. It begins when they start to use objects in the way they are intended to be used. For instance, when given a comb, the child puts it to his head, or he may 'drink' from a cup *but* he will not use the cup to comb his hair. Likewise, you may see children trying to sit on miniature chairs or trying to put dolls' clothes on themselves. Again, they seem to be thinking . . . if this really is a chair, then I can sit on it.

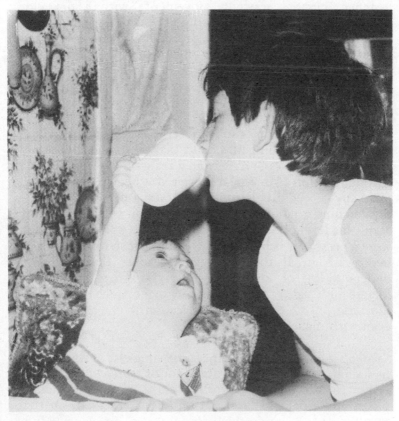

Children show that they recognise objects by doing an appropriate action with them—pushing a car along, putting a spoon into a dish or a shoe on to their foot. Once your child regularly uses objects appropriately, then he can link their names with the meanings he has acquired. But the knowing must be there first.

Children's learning does not stop there—indeed it must not. The next development is when they begin to pretend more wholeheartedly.

This may take the form of adding sounds to the action, such as 'broom-broom' noises as the child pushes the car, slurping noises when drinking from an empty cup or making 'shushing' noises while carefully cradling a doll. The child might also add more detail to his actions, so that the pretence is clearer—for instance, circular washing movements with a dry cloth; deliberate stirring of spoon in a cup or dish; or getting into his usual sleeping position before pretending to be asleep. In all these instances, the child has embellished the simple action with extra details. He has remembered the actions he has seen other people do or, indeed, the actions he has experienced in real life, and can now recreate them in his play. His understanding is now quite advanced.

These developments can be observed or 'tested' even more clearly when watching the child play with a doll or teddy. Incidentally, this can range from a realistic-looking baby doll, through Action-Man type dolls to teddy bears and rag dolls. In sum, any object that is supposed to be a person.

Watching a child playing with the doll will tell you much about his level of understanding. Does he hold it as though it were a person or baby? Will he feed it, brush its hair, put it to bed, wash it? If the child can do these things, then his understanding of common events is well developed. Words like 'drink', 'sleep', 'wash' will now make much more sense to him. He knows these actions because he can recreate them, even with make-believe people.

Symbols—The child has learnt something else as well. He now realises that one object can stand for or *represent* another. For instance, that a piece of stuffed cloth, with a few dangling pieces and a painted face, can represent a person. Or that a cardboard box can be a bath or a lollipop stick a spoon.

This may seem nothing special to you, but for the young baby it is a major achievement—some would say a uniquely human one. What it means is that the child ignores the evidence in front of his eyes and all that he has learnt in past phases and mentally says to himself: 'I see and know that this is a box, but I'm going to imagine that it's a bath.' The capacity to think in terms of symbols, such as the box symbolising the bath, develops gradually. Initially the symbol must be very like the real thing before the child will use it. Children pretend first to drink from real cups, then dolls' tea-sets and later still plastic tubs. At a later stage they may use a completely different object as though it were a cup—e.g. a model car—or they may be content to mime the action without any object.

Pictures of objects are also symbols; they are not the real thing. If children are not at the stage of understanding symbols, then they treat pictures or books like any other object and explore them by mouthing, crumpling or tearing.

When they recognise pictures in terms of what they show—a photograph of Mummy or a picture of a dog—then you know the ability to understand symbols has begun.

Finally, language is a system of sound symbols. Our words stand for or represent the real thing. It is only when children begin to think in symbols that most spoken language starts to make sense to them.

Phase 4: Sequences
The final phase we shall consider in the growth of understanding is the one during which children link their actions into sequences. This is best seen in pretend play, when they sustain the pretence for longer periods.

The earliest sequences tend to involve the same 'pretend' action being done to several people. For instance, the child feeds the doll, then himself, then mummy or anyone else who willingly joins in the game.

Or the child may link different actions around a common theme. For example, he will first put a 'pillow' on the bed, then a doll on the bed with its head on the pillow, then finally cover it with a 'sheet'. Thus three different actions are linked in logical order.

Early sequences will consist of only two or three actions, but later these develop into more complex routines with long strings of actions linked together—the dolls have dinner, then get bathed before going to bed, and so on. The children will play without any prompts or help from other people, often totally absorbed in their own make-believe world.

You can see evidence of sequences in other play activities—the child building a house or a bridge from bricks, drawing a picture or solving a puzzle. The one feature they all have in common is that the child must plan ahead if he is to achieve the desired result.

Mental planning—If your child is able to plan ahead, then he has entered this phase of understanding. Here are a couple of ways in which you can test whether your child has a plan in mind as he plays.

* Does your child break off play to search for an appropriate object and immediately resume when he has found it? For example, he has undressed the doll, put it in a bath and then looks for something to act as a face cloth. Once found, he immediately resumes play by washing the doll. In short, he knew what he wanted and he was not side-tracked.
* Does the child resist your attempts to change the game? The doll is having a bath and you come along with a tea-pot and try to feed it. Or Action Man is driving around in his jeep (a shoe box) and you try to wash him. Protests from the child suggest you are interfering with his plans.
  Conversely, if you correctly anticipate what the child wants to happen next, then he will let you join in the play. So it is not just a case of him wanting to play alone.

Language, too, involves mental planning. Not only do we have to think of what it is we want, we also have to recall its name. Equally, when it comes to stringing words together in sentences, we have to plan mentally what we are going to say: 'dolly . . . drive . . . car . . . shops.'

There is plenty of evidence that children must to able to produce sequences in their play before they will talk in meaningful sentences.

Summary

The phases in children's growth of understanding are summarised in the Table overleaf. The three columns tell you:

* First, the understandings that children have about particular objects.
* Second, what they have learnt about objects in general.
* Third, the main implications that this has for language and learning to talk.

We must stress, however, that this picture is very much simplified. In reality, it can be quite difficult to determine precisely what phase each child is at. Remember, we are having to guess what is going on inside his head.

Another reason for our difficulty is that children do not progress smoothly from one phase to another. Rather, one phase will still be developing when another begins.

As Fig. 4 shows (p. 95), the child's understanding is something like a cone filled with four flavours of ice-cream. Instead of being neatly layered, one on top of the other, each layer or phase overlaps. Thus, as you 'grow' up the cone, before all the 'exploring' flavour is finished, the relating phase begins (point 1). Later—at point 2—some sequences have started and yet, looking ahead, there's more pretending, relating and exploring still to come.

Therefore, when you observe your child, you should expect to see signs of understanding from different levels. The important thing is to know what is *typical* for your child, a point we shall come back to later.

Finally, there will come a point—such as point 3 on the diagram—when a child has completely passed through a phase—in this instance 'exploring' has finished. What this means is that the child has no further need to explore. Straight away he knows about an object, merely by looking at it. However, when faced with an unusual object, he could easily revert to exploring actions. The point is, he no longer needs to do so regularly; the exploring phase has served its purpose. A similar occurrence is with crawling. Once the child can walk competently, he no longer crawls, although he could do so if necessary.

TABLE 3.1: Summary of phases in children's understanding

Phase	Children's actions with objects	Knowledge of objects	Implication for language
1 *Exploring*	Discovers the physical properties of objects—how they differ	Knows objects exist even though the child no longer sees or feels them	No understanding of object names. Only produces playful sounds as though the child is exploring with his voice
2 *Relations*	Discovers the various ways in which objects relate to one another; repeats these actions	Understands that objects can be used as a means to achieve desired end	Links own sounds/words to repeated actions. Understanding grows of words like 'in', 'off', 'out'
3 *Pretending*	Recognises objects with an appropriate action. Later adds extra details such as noises or gestures which represent further the action the child recreates	Uses one object to stand for or as a symbol of another. This can be a life-like object, or a toy or a picture	Now understands and uses words for object names and later for the actions the child performs
4 *Sequences*	Links different objects and play actions into a sustained sequence with a theme running throughout	Able to plan ahead and can order objects and the actions associated with them into logical sequences. Best seen in pretend play with dolls, etc.	Follows instructions which involve two or more objects/events—'Put teddy to bed'. Starts to combine words into short sentences

The growth of Understanding

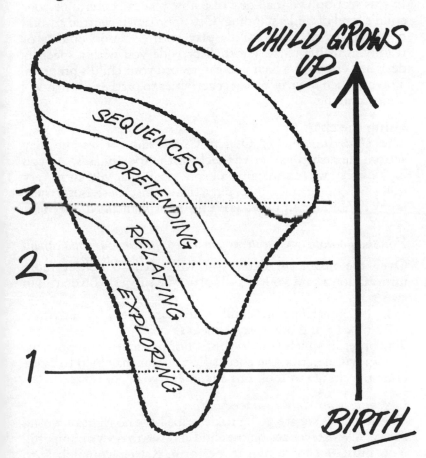

CHILD GROWS UP

SEQUENCES

PRETENDING

RELATING

EXPLORING

3

2

1

BIRTH

GET SET

ASSESSING YOUR CHILD'S UNDERSTANDING OF OBJECTS

In this section, we shall describe how you can determine your child's level of understanding. Our approach is centred around observations of your child's play with common objects or readily available toys. We shall provide you with a specially designed chart on which you can record your child's progress. You can then use this to select activities to further your child's understanding.

Using the chart

The *Understanding of Objects* Chart summarises the play actions described earlier for each of the four phases. As you look over it, we're sure you will spot items that you know very well your child can do. If so, put a tick against these. But if there is any doubt in your mind, leave the item blank until you check it out.

You should now tick the items you are confident your child can do

Over the next few days, you will need to collect more information about your child's play. We suggest you do this in two ways:

    1   by observing your child in ordinary, everyday activities;
    2   by carrying out special checks.

The order in which you do this is not particularly important, but we will describe the checks first as this may help to make clear the things to look out for in everyday contexts.

Checking your child's understandings

The activities we are going to describe have no right or wrong answers. Whatever action the child chooses to do is meaningful. You must *not* force him to perform. Rather your job is to observe what he does. *Interfere as little as possible.*

    The checks consist of providing the child with a collection of toys or objects. We shall suggest three different sets—one each for the phases of exploring, relating and pretending—but you could assemble just one set if your time is limited. All you have to do is to record on the chart the actions which your child performs with the objects. Remember, during the checks the child is allowed to play freely.

We shall then describe some things you might do to test the upper limits of your child's understanding, such as showing your child how to pretend or how to use one object to get another.

Objects to use
The actual objects you use do not matter all that much, provided:
* they are things that the child can handle easily (nothing too big or too small or that would be awkward to position, e.g. plastic dolls);
* the child is reasonably familiar with the objects or they are ones with which he *should* be familiar (out-of-the-ordinary objects are not recommended);
* you present a small number of *different* objects—around six to eight at a time.
To give you some idea of the type of object you might use, here are three sets, each designed to test a particular phase of understanding.

Exploring set—These objects are chosen to encourage a range of exploratory actions, in that they look and feel different. It is best to use objects that are 'new' to the child, although he may have come across others like them. You could pick six objects from the following:
a tennis ball, tea towel, grease-proof paper or crinkly plastic bag *with closed end cut off*, metal spoon, small rag doll, home-made rattle (dried peas in a small plastic bottle or in two yogurt cartons sealed face-to-face), egg whisk (or other metal kitchen tool), child's plastic mirror (N.B. *not* glass mirror), model car, soft squeaky toy, small saucepan and lid.

Relating set—This time, the objects are well suited to the various relational actions that children perform. Of course, this does not preclude them from doing exploratory actions. The following objects are particularly suitable for children who have a well-developed range of exploring actions:
wooden blocks or empty plastic cartons with lids, clothes pegs and plastic bowl, ring-stack type toy, peg-men in 'car', wooden spoon, screw-top jar, small saucepan and lid, tea towel.

UNDERSTANDING OF OBJECTS CHART

Child's Name............................ Date Started................................

PHASE 1 : EXPLORING

Mouths	.....	Others		Object Permanence	
Shakes	.....	....	.....	Reaches round to get toy/object behind back	.....
Hits (holds object hits against floor, wall)	.....	....	.....		
		....	.....	Looks for dropped objects	.....
Examines	.....	....	.....	Removes cloth to obtain object	.....
Feels/rubs	.....	....	.....		
Drops (watches it fall)	.....	....	.....	Empties objects out of container	.....
		....	.....	Obtains object hidden by container (box, cup, etc.)	.....
Throws (watches it fall)	.....	....	.....		
		....	.....		
		....	.....		

PHASE 2 : RELATIONS

Bangs two objects	.....	Relating by use		Means-end Relations	
Places one object into another	.....	Spoon in cup	.....	Dangles toy by string and watches the effect	.....
		Pillow on bed	.....		
Takes rings off stack	.....	Sheet on bed, table	.....	Removes lid from box to get toy/sweet, etc.	.....
Places object on top of another	.....	Moves chair to table	.....	Pulls string to get toy	.....
Builds tower of two cubes	.....	Combs/brushes hair	.....	Pulls cloth to obtain toy	.....
		Lid on teapot/ saucepan	.....	Searches for object hidden under two or more covers	.....
Places rings on stack	.....	Pencil/crayon on paper	.....		
Others		Undresses doll (not carefully)	.....	Uses stick to obtain toy out of reach	.....
....	.....				
....	.....				

UNDERSTANDING OF OBJECTS CHART (Contd.)

PHASE 3 : PRETENDING

				Pictures	
Feeds self/other person with cup	.....	*Dolls*		Kisses pictures of person/teddy	.....
		Feeds with cup	.....		
Feeds self/other person with spoon	.....	Feeds with spoon	.....	Pretends to feed/ wash, etc. picture of person	.....
Makes feeding sounds	.....	Makes feeding sounds	.....		
Washes self	.....	Washes	.....	Pretends to eat foodstuff picture	.....
Sleeps on doll's bed or pillow	.....	Lies doll on bed or pillow	.....	Pretends to drive picture of car (noises)	.....
Sits on doll's chair	.....	Sits doll on chair	.....		
Dresses self with doll's clothes	.....	Undresses/dresses doll (care)	.....		
Others		Combs/brushes doll's hair	.....	*Others*	
....	.....	Hugs/kisses doll	.....	....	.....
....	.....	Walks doll	.....	....	.....
....	.....	Doll jumps	.....	....	.....
....	.....				

PHASE 4 : SEQUENCES

				Imaginary Objects	
Feeds doll/self/ adult	.....	*Same Theme*		Pretend cup/ spoon	.....
		Feeding	.....		
		Sleep	.....		
Combs doll/self/ adult	.....	Bathes	.....	Face-cloth	.....
		Ironing	.....	teapot	.....
Sleeps doll/self/ adult	.....			Copies actions shown on photo/ picture	.....
Telephone doll/ self/adult	.....				
Others		*Others*		*Others*	
....	.....	....	.....	....	.....
....	.....	....	.....	....	.....
....	.....	....	.....	....	.....
....	.....				

Pretending set—The objects we recommend for this phase should encourage children's pretending but we hasten to add that if your child is not at this stage, he or she can still play with them. You will probably see instances of exploring and relating actions with maybe a surprise 'pretend' action. However, this set of toys is mainly for children who are well able to explore and relate objects:

a doll (with easily removed clothing—a rag doll is ideal although Tiny Tears or Action-Man types are also possible)—other soft toys, e.g. 'dog' teddy bear, pretend tea pot, cups, spoon; comb or brush; shoe box (bath, bed, car); margarine tub (table, chair, stool), tea towel, piece of sponge (pillow or face cloth), toy telephone, picture book.

Observing your child

1 You can either select *one* of the three sets which you feel is most suited to the child OR try him or her with all three at *different times* during the week.

2 Choose a time when your child is alert and active and when you are unlikely to be disturbed.

3 Make sure your child is comfortably positioned to play. Sitting on the floor is generally best, but if your child is unable to sit unsupported, you might use a chair with table attached or else prop him or her with cushions on the floor.

4 Lay out the toy selection in front of your child and within easy reach. Stay sitting with the child but wait for him to reach out for an object. Encourage him when he does. By all means talk, laugh, etc—accept whatever he does. DO NOT INTERFERE IN THE PLAY (unless of course he is about to hurt himself.

5 On the *understanding of objects chart*, you can tick off the actions your child performs. Make a new tick every time the child performs the action with a *different* object or comes back to that action after having done another. For instance, a child who throws one clothes peg, then another and another, would get only one tick. If he threw a peg, block and saucepan lid, that would have three ticks. But if he threw a clothes peg, then examined a second peg, mouthed it and then threw it, throwing would be ticked twice and examining and mouthing once.

The idea is to chart the number of *different* actions rather than repetitions of the same action with the same object.

6 Five (5) minutes is probably plenty of time, but if your child wants to continue for longer, you can do so. However, our advice is to stop *before* he gets bored.

7 You can repeat these free-play observations on different days. This will let you see whether your child repeats the same repertoire of actions (which is generally the case) or shows new ones, which means updating your chart, but if an action has already been ticked 10 times or more, you need not bother continuing to record that.

Testing the limits

For the next part of the observation activity, the emphasis changes slightly, in that you should now join in the play. But we suggest you take this slowly and gradually.

1 *Offer an object to the child*—If your child has overlooked an object, hold it out to him and see what he does with it. That is all you have to do.

It is worth doing this if your child gets fixated on one object and plays with nothing else. For example, one boy we know wanted to comb his hair over and over.

At a more advanced level, if the child is in the middle of a pretend sequence, offer him a 'new' object and see if this distracts him. It is a good sign if it does not.

2 *Set the child a problem to solve*—There are some items on the chart which your child is unlikely to show spontaneously, for instance, finding hidden objects.

In this case, you might try taking away an object, hiding it and seeing if your child searches for it. But you are better to wait for a chance, rather than 'forcing' him. For example, if your child drops a toy, cover it with the tea towel. Or if he stretches for something out of reach, put it on a cloth with an end near him and see if he will pull the cloth to retrieve the object.

3 *Play with the objects*—This time, you quite simply start playing with some of the objects yourself—doing actions which you have not seen your child do. For instance, dropping objects in the exploring phase or piling objects on top of one

another in the relating phase or pretending to wash your face. Repeat these actions a number of times—and act as though you are enjoying yourself. Indeed, the more babyish you are, the better. Do not be too concerned if your child keeps doing his own thing; although it is a bonus if he takes time to watch you. DO NOT FORCE HIM TO WATCH. Rather, pick the time when he is likely to attend to you.

Note whether the child starts to copy you.

If he does
* Was his attempt very short-lived and did he soon give up, preferring his own activities? If so, this is a sign that he is just beginning to grasp that idea. He needs many more experiences before he fully understands.
* Did he carry on with your action, possibly extending it to other objects? If so, then your child's understanding is probably well developed. You have merely triggered off an action he had not thought to do but one which he is well capable of doing.

If he does not copy you
* It probably means that your actions were beyond his level of understanding. You could check this by modelling actions from an earlier phase and see whether he now joins in your game.

It is very hard to be definite about a child's level of understanding. Indeed, we often excuse the child by saying, 'he wasn't watching me' or, 'if only he would concentrate more' or, 'he's too distractible'. Sometimes these may be true. On the other hand, we believe that more often these are symptoms of a child's failure to understand. They disappear when he acquires that level of understanding.

Everyday observations
The chart can also be kept up-to-date by adding to it, as you observe your child in everyday activities. For instance, his exploration of the saucepan cupboards while you are doing the dishes may show you that he understands that lids go on pans or that they bang together to make a noise, that you fit one pan inside another—and so forth.

If you pin a copy of the chart up in the kitchen, you can quickly tick off these actions as they occur. It does help, however, to have carried out some 'test' observations, because then you will know what in particular to look for; such as—instances of actions you have not seen him do with the set of special objects but which you are convinced you have observed him do previously.

Or you might test whether the child will perform the action with different sorts of objects. For example, you observed him pretending to drink from his own cup, but will he pretend with another cup or a mug, beaker, etc? Or what does he do if his plaything rolls out of reach under the settee? Will he try to retrieve it with a stick in the way he did during the 'tests'?

Taking stock
Your completed chart may or may not resemble the example we give of a girl called Ciara. At least it shows you one child's record.

Even a quick glance at this, or any completed chart, will tell you three things:
First, the phases which the child does *not* understand. There are few, or no ticks recorded in that section of the chart.
Second, the phases in which the child has well-developed understanding. Here there are many ticks against most, if not all items.
Third, the phases where the child's understanding is still developing. Here, only some items are ticked and even then, there may only be one or two ticks aginst an item.

So, how does your child rate? Write in the names of the four phases under the appropriate headings.

WELL DEVELOPED UNDERSTANDING	UNDERSTANDING IS DEVELOPING	NO UNDERSTANDING

UNDERSTANDING OF OBJECTS CHART

Name...... CIARA .... Date Started...... JANUARY 15th

---

PHASE 1 : EXPLORING

Mouths	////	Others		Object Permanence	
Shakes	///	Squeezes	////		
Hits	////////	Stretches	/	Reaches round to get toy/object behind back	//////
(holds object hits against floor, wall)	.....	Tears	/	Looks for dropped objects	///
Examines	/////////		.....	Removes cloth to obtain object	/////////
Feels/rubs	/////				
Drops (watches it fall)	/////		.....	Empties objects out of container	////////
			.....	Obtains object hidden by container (box, cup, etc.)	////
Throws (watches it fall)	/////////		.....		

PHASE 2 : RELATIONS

Bangs two objects	///////	Relating by use		Means-end Relations	
Places one object into another	////////	Spoon in cup	/////	Dangles toy by string and watches the effect	//////
		Pillow on bed	.....		
Takes rings off stack	/////////	Sheet on bed, table	.....	Removes lid from box to get toy/sweet, etc.	/////
Places object on top of another	//	Moves chair to table	.....	Pulls string to get toy	///
Builds tower of two cubes	//	Combs/brushes hair	////////	Pulls cloth to obtain toy	/
Places rings on stack	//	Lid on teapot/ saucepan	//	Searches for object hidden under two or more covers	///////
Others		Pencil/crayon on paper	////////	Uses stick to obtain toy out of reach	.....
Pegs into hole	/////	Undresses doll (not carefully)	.....		
Formboard	///				

UNDERSTANDING OF OBJECTS CHART (Contd.)

PHASE 3 : PRETENDING

		Dolls		*Pictures*	
Feeds self/other person with cup	//////.///	Feeds with cup	//	Kisses pictures of person/teddy	.//
Feeds self/other person with spoon	/////////	Feeds with spoon	///////	Pretends to feed/ wash, etc. picture of person	///
Makes feeding sounds	.....	Makes feeding sounds	.....		
Washes self	///...	Washes	.....	Pretends to eat foodstuff picture	.....
Sleeps on doll's bed or pillow	.....	Lies doll on bed or pillow	.....	Pretends to drive picture of car (noises)	.....
Sits on doll's chair	../...	Sits doll on chair	/		
Dresses self with doll's clothes	.....	Undresses/dresses doll (care)	.....		
Others		Combs/brushes doll's hair	////////	*Others*	
Telephone to ear- 'talks'	///////	Hugs/kisses doll	//	Licks lollipop picture	/
Tries to get into	//...	Walks doll	.....		.....
'Action-Man' Jeep	.....	Doll jumps	.....		

PHASE 4 : SEQUENCES

		Same Theme		*Imaginary Objects*	
Feeds doll/self/ adult	../.	Feeding	.....	Pretend cup/ spoon	.....
		Sleep	.....		
Combs doll/self/ adult	//...	Bathes	.....	Face-cloth	.....
		Ironing	.....	teapot	.....
Sleeps doll/self/ adult	.....			Copies actions shown on photo/ picture	.....
Telephone doll/ self/adult	.....				
Others		*Others*		*Others*	
Places people in car	///		.....		.....
	.....		.....		.....
	.....		.....		.....
	.....		.....		.....

Do not be surprised if all four phases are listed in the same column—it can happen. Remember the way the four flavours intermingled in the ice-cream cone? (p. 95).

The important column, to our way of thinking, is the *middle one*. We believe you have to begin with what your child is presently doing and extend it. Hence, phases listed under 'No understanding' are too far advanced as yet. They will start to emerge once the earlier phases are better established.

Finally, you should look more closely at the items you ticked on the chart for the phases you have listed as still developing. This time we want you to group the items into *strengths* (those observed often and with different sorts of objects) and *weaknesses* (those with few or no ticks). You can do this for each of the phases you have identified, but we suggest you start with the two most basic ones, i.e. exploring and relating or relating and pretending or pretending and sequencing. With very young or severely handicapped children you might only need to do this for the *exploring* phase, whereas with older or more advanced children *sequencing* could be the only phase you need to analyse.

Armed with this information, you can start to read about ways of developing your child's understanding.

Phase..............		Phase..............	
Strengths	*Weaknesses*	*Strengths*	*Weaknesses*

GO

DEVELOPING CHILDREN'S UNDERSTANDING

Our suggestions are grouped according to the four phases (see pp. 85–92). Although you need only read those which are of direct concern to your child at present, we suggest you try to get the flavour of each, as this will let you see where you have come from and where you are going.

Each section contains specific ideas for toys and activities you might use. However, these listings are by no means exhaustive and we depend on you to think of others. Inspiration comes best, we find, from discussing ideas with other people, by tapping each other's brains at a group meeting or enlisting the family's help. Brothers and sisters are often very inventive if given a chance.

First, though, we want to summarise the limited number of ways adults can be of assistance. Remember, it is the children who have to do the understanding. We cannot *make* them, nor can we do it for them. At best, we can provide *opportunities* that will let their understanding grow. Among the more important ones are the following:

* *Varied experiences*—This not only means being given different sorts of objects to play with—and not just what we adults call toys—but also the chance to experience different environments and to be involved in activities both around the house and outside it.

* *Active children*—Enabling the children to do as much as possible for themselves is very important. For example, attaching a string to a mobile and then tying the other end loosely around the child's arm or leg, will let him discover the connection between his movement and the visual event. Older children who cannot yet walk, can explore if they are placed in baby-walkers. These are but two examples of how we can let children be more active explorers.

* *Make their own discoveries*—Children also learn better if they are left to make their own discoveries. At the simplest level this means giving them time to look for dropped objects

or to think of how they might get an object that is out of reach. If necessary, you might give them a clue—shaking the tin to let them know the object is still inside—and wait to see if they respond. Finding out for yourself is a better way of learning than having someone do it for you.

* *Watching you*—At the pretending and sequencing level, one very good way for children to learn is through watching you play with the pretend toys. So join in with your child, keep your actions in tune with his or her play—nothing too imaginative at first. This is just as important for boys as it is for girls, and fathers are every bit as good teachers as mothers. Indeed, other brothers and sisters can join in as well.

Nor does this only apply to pretending. You should make a point of showing your child 'new' things to do with toys and objects. In this instance we mean new to them. Your child may end up doing the same as you—washing dishes, loading the washing machine, helping with the dusting. This 'practice' will certainly further their understanding, even if it fails to lighten your workload straight away.

* *Encouragement*—We all need an incentive to keep trying and young babies are no different. Your attention is probably the best encouragement and if you show how pleased you are with your child's *attempts* (note attempts, not just successes), then it is likely he will keep trying.

Nor should you demand too much too soon. The satisfaction of getting what you want is another important source of encouragement. Hence, if the child is struggling to free an object from a cloth, don't let it go on too long. Your encouragement may not stave off the frustration that is bound to build up. Too much of it will discourage the child from trying.

The key points, then, to remember in developing children's understanding are:
* Varied experiences
* Active children
* Making discoveries
* Encouragement.

Now for some suggestions to further children's learning within each of the four phrases. You should pay particular attention to the phases you identified in the last activity and be on the look-out particularly for suggestions to overcome your child's weaknesses.

We first list simple activities suitable for young babies or very handicapped children. More advanced activities are suggested for older and more able children.

Exploring

Simple activities

Hold toys in front of child and slowly move from side to side

Dangle toys on elastic string in front of the child

Mobiles—hung over cot or near baby chair. Can be home-made

Musical mobile—plays tune as shapes rotate

Attach string from mobile to child's arm—as he moves, the mobile moves

Home-made rattles—plastic bottles filled with rice, chestnuts, etc.

Play with paper—brown paper bags, greaseproof or computer paper

Cot and pram toys—on elastic or rod

Wobble-globes—rattles, etc. on suction base

Activity Bear (Matchbox)

Activity Centre (Fisher-Price)

Baby Action Ball (Playskool)—easily gripped and beads move inside

Colourful mittens with bells sewn on (likewise socks)

Dropping toys into tin box or into water

Unwrapping toy in newspaper

Hammering on tin box, etc.

Bath-time toys—floating on water

Cloth bricks

Knocking over a tower of bricks

Pulling string on toy to make music play or to move arms and legs of figure

Squeaky toys

Drum

Xylophone

Water play—bath time, sink or baby bath on floor

Junk box—containers of various shapes and sizes

Rag-bag—filled with scraps of materials. Child feels before seeing

More advanced activities

Shopping bag—emptying unbreakables

Cupboard searches—special place for child to explore novel things

Making shapes with Play dough clay or home-made flour dough

Finger painting (Blowing bubbles in water—making foam

Sand play—sieves, chutes, wheel turning, etc.

Smelling—cotton wool balls with liquids on them—after-shave, peppermint essence, etc.

Tasting—small bites of strong tasting foods

Relating

Simple activities

Putting toys into a container

Placing chunky peg-men into car, boats, etc.

Rings on to simple ring-stack

Simple post boxes—four shapes

Hiding toys under clothes or in boxes, etc.

Posting small toys down cardboard tubes

Pulling string to get toys out of reach—tie wool to child's favourite toys

'Treasure hunt'—wrap toy in paper then hide in box, cover box with cloth, etc.

Dangle balloon on string over table—child pulls string to make balloon appear

Tunnel pegs

Hammer balls/pegs

Shape sorter—Fisher-Price

Ring-stack—Fisher-Price

Building beakers

Nesting boxes

Tower of bricks

Simple formboards—six pieces

Pop-up cones—'Trigger-Jigger'

Peg boards

Filling up containers with small objects—pebbles, chestnuts, shells, etc.

More advanced activities
Threading beads on to lace—with wooden 'needle' on end of lace at first

Inset boards—10+ pieces

Sorts shapes in postbox —10+

Unscrews tops from bottles and jars

Billy and his Barrels (Kiddicraft) unscrews and orders by size

Russian dolls—they nest inside one another

Wind-up clockwork toy

Duplo Lego—connects and takes apart

Giant snap-lock beads (Fisher-Price)

Squeeze-bulb toys—e.g. make a frog jump

Jack-in-the-box

Stickle bricks

Spoons rice, peas, lentils, etc., from one container to another

Throwing games—skittles, bean bags in boxes, large hoopla

Making puppet appear and disappear—behind back, underneath pullovers, etc.

Pretending
Rag Dolls

Soft toys—teddy, animals, etc.

Tea sets, plates, pretend food, etc.

Pretend furniture—bed, table, chair—made from wood or cardboard boxes

Car, trains, fire engines that people fit into

Doll's buggy, pram or cradle

Pretend iron, ironing board, baking sets, telephones, washing up bowl, etc.

Steering wheel and model dashboard of car

Simple train set, push-along

Model carpet sweeper, lawn-mower

Safety mirror—recognises reflections

Picture cubes—made from boxes, foam, etc.

Family photographs on cubes or in small albums

Simple picture books—making pretend noises with pictures of animals

Ladybird picture books or similar

Picture cards—finds two the same, etc.

Pretend actions when reading story to child

Pretending to be a dog, cat—adult makes noises and walks around

Children copy you with real objects, e.g. when polishing, brushing floor, etc.

Hunts for hidden toy, i.e. child closes eyes when it is being hidden, then change over

Sequences

Action Man and jeep, heli-copter, etc.

Sindy or Barbie doll and accessories

Doll's house

Model garage, farm, play-ground

Playpeople sets—nurses, builders (miniature figures)

Duplo characters and accessories

Fabuland figures and accessories (Lego)

Wooden blocks—builds houses, pretend village, etc.

Large roadways—play mats with streets drawn out, etc.

Pretend cooker with model saucepans, etc.

Wendy House—can be made from large cardboard box

Pretend cars, boats, etc., made from cardboard boxes

Dressing up clothes—shoes, hats, etc.

Rejoins cut-up picture or photograph (two or three pieces at first and then more)

Cash register, scales, etc., for pretend shop

Hand puppets

Finger puppets

Ladybird Talkabout series of books—home, school, garden, etc.

Children retelling familiar story through mime

Simple charades—'guess what I'm doing?' (e.g. drinking), 'who am I?' (e.g. driver)

Dressing up sets—nurses, bus conductors, postman

Making and wearing hats—
pirates, a king's crown, etc.

Simple jig-saws—six-plus
pieces

Fighting with pretend
swords, riding pretend
horses, etc.

Drawing 'People', 'house'

Ideas to try
Activity The final activity in this section requires you to list
some new 'games' or play activities to try out with your child.
We suggest you list three or four activities for each 'phase' of
understanding you wish to develop.

Phase..............	Phase..............
The activities I am going to try are:	The activities I am going to try are:

Over the next week or so, try these out with your child.
Remember:
* *Follow your child's interests*—be an opportunist; take your
* lead from the child and be prepared to change your plans
  according to the child's reactions.
* *Choose your time*—when your child is likely to be attentive
  and you are feeling up to it.
* *Stop while the going's good*—do not let the activity go on until
  the child gets bored. It is better to stop when the children are
  enjoying it, so that they will look forward to it again.
* *Simplify the activity*—children need to experience success
  more often than failure. Can you make the game simpler so
  that the child can manage to do it? Later you can gradually
  make it more difficult.

* *Play it again, chum!*—do not be put off if your child shows little interest in the new activity. Have another go a day or so later. Equally, the children may demand to 'do it again'. If so, you will have been successful at introducing your child to new play activities.

You should not expect to see any major changes in your child's behaviour immediately. Understanding develops slowly. Be on the look-out for signs that it is growing and continue to give your child opportunities to learn. Keep your charts up-to-date.

* You can cross off some of the weaknesses you listed on the table on page 106.
* New behaviours can be added to the Understanding of Objects chart (p. 98).
* You might start working on a new phase of understanding.

This should give you encouragement, because invariably there will be times when you wonder if your child is making any progress at all and you may feel powerless to do anything more. If you ever feel like this, rest assured you have probably done all you can. It is now up to the child. More often than not, your patience will be rewarded before too long.

Finally, we outline some ideas as to how you might deal with 'problems' which parents frequently encounter, especially with older handicapped children.

Throwing
Ask yourself: 'Why is the child doing it? Habit, to get attention or through frustration? Depending on your answer you could:

a) Ignore, when it is for attention, but do ensure that you attend to the child when he or she is playing appropriately;
b) firm '*No*' before the child throws;
c) use toys which cannot be thrown, i.e. ones fastened by clamps to table or wall;
d) introduce child to new activities that are more fun.

Throwing can take some time to eliminate if it has become a habit. However it is a natural play action for young babies and is only gradually replaced as the child acquires other actions.

Mouthing

This, too, is a natural play action with babies. For some severely physically handicapped or blind children, mouthing is a useful way for them to learn about the world. However, some handicapped children persist in mouthing objects with the result that they do little else.

In general, however, you need to encourage children to discover other exploratory actions. Get them using their hands more to explore; vary the textures, objects and the materials you give them, e.g. sand—that does not taste very nice! Or introduce them to toys which are interesting to look at, such as spinning tops, and show them how they can use objects to make noises.

Mouthing will gradually disappear as the child plays more.

Won't play with anything else

Some children seem to get obsessed with one particular toy or activity and it is difficult to persuade them to play with anything else. Indeed, they may well derive quite a bit of comfort from their repetitive play. Hence you should introduce variation gradually and try pairing new toys with the familiar ones. In time the child may well come to prefer some of the new things you have introduced

Destroying toys

Handicapped children are more physically mature than their level of play. They break toys designed for younger, non-handicapped children. One solution is, buy or borrow more robust wooden toys.

If children are breaking toys deliberately—perhaps to gain attention—then remove the toy and leave them without anything for ten minutes or so. Bring back the toy; praise and encourage as long as they play with it appropriately. However, remove it straight away if they go to damage it again.

Will not sit still

When introducing new activities and toys, keep it short, model play for the child and ensure he sits down before having a turn. Stop the game if the child gets up and runs around. Take a break before re-introducing the game. Over a period you should be able to increase the length of time the child spends playing.

Not interested in toys
The toys which are guaranteed to interest nearly every child (and adult) are those that produce a big effect for little effort. For example, if the child touches the toy, lights come on and bells ring. These devices can be added to existing toys or built into specially designed ones. From these beginnings children's interest in the toys can be nurtured.

SECTION FOUR: TAKING TURNS

In Section Two we looked at the messages children send, including those in the early months of life that are *not intentional*. Before the child sends intentional messages, he must *know* what he wants, whether it is food or a toy or a particular shirt to wear. This means he must understand the objects and actions that he wants to talk about. We dealt with the development of this understanding in *Section Three*.

There are other skills required in sending intentional messages. The child has to learn how to get on with other people. This is sometimes called learning to *interact* with them or *taking turns*. All babies acquire the skills of interacting long before they talk. This section will tell you how they do it.

What you will read about in this section

ON YOUR MARKS

Preverbal conversations. We explain how children's understanding of objects and events links with their growing ability to interact with the important people in their lives to provide the basis for *intentional* communications. We also describe what is involved in a conversation and how young infants can 'converse' with their mums and dads, even though they cannot say a word.

Three essential preverbal skills. We highlight three essential skills for children to master: *looking together* (attending to people and objects), *imitation* (copying other people's actions) and *turn-taking* (in simple games and routines). Together these form the foundation for later learning of skills in language, speech and communication.

GET SET

Assessing preverbal skills. We describe how you can assess your child's turn-taking abilities and provide you with simple checklists to aid your observations and help you keep a record of the stage your child has reached.

GO

Play activities to encourage preverbal skills. The simple games that parents usually play with babies are an ideal way for learning to take place. We describe a variety of games that have proved popular with the parents we know. You should pick up new ideas for games here.

At the end of this section we also explain how children move from *preverbal* to *verbal* communication and how you can help your child by adding sounds and then words to your games.

ON YOUR MARKS

PREVERBAL CONVERSATIONS

Meaningful conversations between a parent and child can take place long before the child can talk. There are three essential ingredients in these conversations.

1 *An understanding of objects and events in the child's environment*
Before a child can 'talk' he must have a *reason* to talk and something to talk about. The things that children talk about first are those things that affect them closely in their everyday lives, the objects and events that take place each day; like having breakfast, bathtime, playing with their brothers and sisters. But before they can talk about these things, they have to *understand* the objects and events with which they are involved. We discussed in Section Three how they achieve this.

2 *Interactions with significant people in the child's everyday life*
Talking is necessary because we live in communities with other people and we want to be able to share our needs and feelings with them. Children, such as the famous boy of Aveyron who was reared by wolves until he was ten years old and did not learn to talk until he was found and cared for by humans, highlight the very important role that care-givers have in helping the child learn to communicate. As we explained in Section Two, they do this first by being *responsive* to the child's needs, even though his early communications are not intentional. So the child becomes an *active participant* in social exchanges and gradually learns that his sounds and gestures *cause* certain other things to happen. In this way, he is motivated to *want* to communicate and, gradually, as a result of these experiences, he learns that *specific* sounds and/or *specific* gestures get *specific* responses from those caring for him. He now knows that there is a shared system of signs that can be used to communicate his meaning to others. Instead of crying, he can raise his arms if he wishes to be lifted up and, later, he learns that he can achieve the same effect by using the word 'up!' In all three cases, the most likely response is that his mother will lift him up and say 'There—is that better?' or, 'Do

you want to come up now?' The child may stop crying or make a sound of pleasure, perhaps pat the mother's face or make a new demand—to see out of the window or to have his mother set his coloured mobile swinging. Here we have the beginnings of a *conversation*.

3 What is involved in taking part in a conversation?

A conversation is deceptively simple because, as adults, we are so used to conversing that it is easy to overlook the complexity of the skills required. The early *sounds* that children make do not automatically lead to conversational skills. It is only when these sounds become part of interactive games and routines that they develop conversational meanings. It is through involving the child in early games, nursery rhymes or other ritual activities, that the care-giver teaches the child the rules involved in a conversation.

Here are two examples of early conversations; one begun by a mother; the second by a child.

a) 'Hello'—mother leans over cot.
    'Goo'—baby smiles at mother.
    'Do you want your teddy?'—mother holds teddy in front of child.
    'Ah'—child reaches for teddy.
    'There he is!'—mother puts teddy in child's hand.

b) 'Eh!'—child points at cat sitting on window ledge.
    'That's Tibby, he wants his dinner.'
    'Ah?'—child puts his hand out to the door and looks at mother.
    'Shall we let him in, then?'—mother waits for child's response.
    Child nods his head.
    'There we are, then!'—mother opens door.

Let us look more closely at what is involved in carrying on even simple conversations such as these.

* *The sender of the message (parent or child) has to decide:*
    —Have I got something worth saying? Can I be bothered to say it?
    —Who am I going to send the message to?
    —What message shall I send? What shall I tell them?

—How shall I convey the message—through gesture or sounds or words, or a combination of the three?

Some of the problems that senders commonly run into, are:

—The person they are talking to is too busy with other things and does not pay attention;

—The message does not interest the listener, who stops attending to it;

—The sender does not realise that his message is unclear; his gestures, sounds or words do not make sense to the other person.

These three difficulties can happen to children as well as parents.

* *The sender has to wait for a response*

Once the sender has taken a turn, he has to wait for the 'receiver' to reply. Better still, he should signal that his message has ended so that the receiver knows it is his turn.

Problems—The most common problem that infants experience is that their parents do not give them enough time to reply. They rush on to a new message too soon.

The problem some parents face is that their children do not leave long enough pauses in their conversation, either—they are constantly making sounds, gestures, etc.

* *The receiver of the message has to:*

—attend to the sender's message;

—work out what it means;

—respond appropriately to it.

Among the problems which 'receivers' encounter are:

—Deciding whether the sender is trying to communicate with them or not. It is not always clear with young infants.

—Knowing the meaning of the sender's signals. The more familiar they are with the sender, the easier this is.

—The sender does not mean what he ways, or he does not say what he means. For instance, a mother says to a child, 'Would you like to go for a walk in the park?' The child learns that he can answer this by 'saying' 'Yes' or 'No' (either in gestures or words). But when mother says, 'Would you like to put your toys away now?' there really is no choice. What she means is, 'Do it—don't answer me back.'

* *The sender becomes the receiver and the receiver becomes the sender*

Once the receiver has understood the message, he may send back a reply—or indicate that he heard but does not wish to continue the conversation. He may instead start a new topic.

In the above examples, the conversation cycle continues because the two people take it in turns to *send and receive* messages. Sometimes the replies carry on the same theme. At other times, new topics are introduced into the conversation.

Infants can find this switching difficult. The best help is a responsive care-giver who is quick to respond to his not-very-expertly sent messages and, equally, leaves him time to respond to the messages she has sent him.

To summarise, then, early conversations grow out of the child's
* *understanding* of objects and events in his everyday life;
* *interactions* with the significant people in his life;
* learning to *take turns* in sending messages, responding to messages and switching quickly between the two.

THREE ESSENTIAL PREVERBAL SKILLS
From earliest infancy babies begin to acquire three very important skills which, *together*, form a foundation for learning to talk because they are skills needed for conversation.

* *Looking together*—the skill of attending to people and objects.
* *Imitation*—the skill of imitating other people's actions, gestures, expressions and sounds.
* *Turn-taking*—the skill of taking turns in simple games and action routines with one other person.

We shall describe these skills from their *earliest* beginnings up to more *advanced* levels. In acquiring all three, the main driving force is the infant's care-giver. Despite his helplessness and inability to converse, the baby's care-givers—mother and father—are attentive and responsive to his needs and enjoy playing and interacting with him during his wakeful periods. These may seem too ordinary to be important, yet without this grounding, babies would not know how to get on with other people.

Looking together—the skill of attending to people and objects

Invariably we look at people when we are talking to them. Likewise, if you are talking about something—a picture, say—you look at it, as well as your listener, switching your gaze between the two.

Equally, the listener has to look at the *speaker* and at the things being talked about. If he does not *look*, the speaker gets the strong impression that he is not listening. Babies have to learn the skill of looking at people and objects as they 'talk'.

Early stages—The first step is *mutual gazing*, where the baby looks intently at the mother's face and she at his. If his gaze shifts to some other object, she is likely to shift hers, too, to see what he is looking at. As the infant grows, he learns that he can *direct* his mother's attention by looking first at her and then at an object that interests him. He does this long before he can point or use a word to refer to the object. The mother, too, uses the same procedure to direct his attention—looks first at the baby and then at the object. It is likely that she will also point to, touch or stroke the object as well as referring to it verbally.

This 'game' of mutual looking can be played with all sorts of objects or events. For instance, the child's attention may be drawn by his mother's hair or nose, or it may be the softness of her jumper or the shiny button on her shirt. She will respond by following his gaze and touching her hair or his hand, or rubbing his hand against her jumper, or pointing to her button and saying 'soft' or 'shiny'. By following the child's attention as he looks at each object, she *encourages* his interest and gives him more information about the objects and events in his world as they catch his attention. And all this can occur during everyday routine activities, or through playtime games, such as clapping hands and hiding hands over faces.

These early experiences of sharing attention and looking together are *mutually satisfying*. Mums and dads enjoy them as much as the child.

Advanced stages—In the early stages, the parents followed the child's gaze and focused on what interested him. A more advanced stage comes when the child can follow his parents'

interests and look with them at the same object or event. The parents can *direct* the child's attention. This comes about through the parents and the children *doing* things together. It is not very interesting for children merely to watch while mum or dad do all the exciting things. Children much prefer to be taking part. It ensures that they are looking at and experiencing what you, the parents, are talking about.

Take an activity like washing dishes. Children who can have a go at doing it will have a much better idea of what you are talking about when you say, 'wet', 'hot', 'wash', 'drips', 'splash', than the child who merely watches or sees a picture. This is true for all sorts of activities, be they in the house, garden or neighbourhood. Doing things together with someone you know well gives you both *something* to talk about, *someone* to talk to and a *reason* for talking.

Early imitation—the skill of imitating simple actions
All children are copy-cats. It is a great way of learning new things, but the ability to imitate has to develop gradually. It is not present from birth and it will not suddenly appear.

Early stages—In the same way that the mother follows the infant's gaze, so she watches and encourages his movements—how he waves his fists, or pokes his tongue out. If she imitates the child's actions or sounds, it is possible to turn his random behaviour into a *game* which they can share, because it is highly likely that the child will imitate her actions—after all, he did them in the first place! As the child matures and learns a wider range of skills, these early copying routines develop into more complicated action sequences for games, such as clap hands, peek-a-boo and dropping the rattle for someone to retrieve it. Children are often willing to continue these much-loved activities indefinitely, delighting in their ability to imitate and have you imitate them. After a while, it is hard to know which is which.

Advanced stages—Once we can imitate what other people *do*, then we have a means of learning how to do *new* things that we have never done before, and of practising the same things over and over. If the child sees you *point* to the pictures on each page as you look at your book together, it will probably not be long before he is pointing, too.

In the same way, he will learn to *shake* the powder, to *pull up* his pants, to *eat* with a spoon, to *roll* a ball and to *kiss* daddy good night—in fact all the actions that make up his daily routine. He will not learn them all at once, but if you do a lot of things together and you have the time to do the new things slowly, he will *want* to do them, too—and he will imitate you.

Later he will learn to *mix* the dough and *roll* it into a ball or to *cut* the flowers (if his hands are able to manage scissors).

If he is used to learning by *doing* things that you do, then, when it comes to learning more difficult things, like saying specific sounds and words, he will probably try to *say* what you say as well. That is why American children speak English with one accent and Australian children have another.

Early turn-taking—the skill of taking turns in simple games

We have already seen the importance of taking turns in conversations—having your say, waiting, letting the other person have a go, then responding. These skills do not come easily to a baby who is not used to waiting or watching and who wants to be active. Practice comes during play-time with mum or dad.

Early stages—Early copying games are the starting point of learning to take turns. For instance, the child pokes out his tongue or moves his hands together. The care-giver takes the second turn by copying the child's actions. If this appeals to the baby, he will repeat his action, thereby taking another turn, which the parent again copies, and so on. As these games are fun, the child gets plenty of practice, even learning to wait between turns or to do more complicated actions or to start the game when you suggest it. Even in this early stage, he learns to:

* *wait* or hold back his actions so that the other person has the time to do something. Some children can find this very difficult;
* *watch* what the other person does and/or says;
* *alter* his actions according to what he has seen or heard.

These are the three elements involved in turn-taking. Every baby has to master them, first with one person, usually a parent who is prepared to put up with his poor attempts at turn-taking, and then later with groups of children.

Advanced stages—Later on, learning to take turns in a shared activity with someone you like is not so difficult if:

1   they expect you to take a turn, and
2   they give you a little bit of help.

For example, if dad turned a page in the book, he could say, 'Your turn,' and help the child get his finger in the right place and not mind too much if two pages got turned over together. Later, you and your child can take turns mixing the dough and using the cutter to press out the shapes. Your child may not be so keen to give it back, but if you say 'My turn now' and put your hand out, he will probably give it to you—especially if he knows that you will give it back to him again for his next go.

You can also play games where turns are necessary, such as rolling or throwing the ball to each other or throwing bean bags into a box. From here, co-operative activities become possible— helping you unload the shopping, putting cutlery into the right sections of the drawer, tidying up the room. All these non-verbal skills will be needed when it comes to conversation.

Summary

1   *Early looking together* grows out of the parent's *responsiveness* to the infant's behaviour—following his gaze, focusing on what he is attending to and later directing his attention. Through this, the child learns to *attend* to objects and activities with another person.

2   *Early imitation* grows out of the early *games* parents play with the infant, such as imitating his actions. Gradually he learns to imitate new actions in early play routines and games, or in everyday activities. More complicated actions, like making certain speech sounds, then become possible.

3   *Early turn-taking* begins with copying games, but these develop into shared activities in which the child takes an active role, taking his turn and then waiting for his next one. Gradually he learns to take turns in games with other partners.

These three skills are the building blocks for taking part in social conversation.

GET SET

ASSESSING PREVERBAL SKILLS

Can your child:

a) *attend* together during an object or activity with you?

b) *imitate* simple actions in a game or routine activity with you?

c) *take turns* with you in a game or routine activity?

In order to answer these questions, you need to *observe* what your child does in a variety of situations during the course of your everyday activities. Be sure to provide him with *opportunities* to 'look together' with you, to imitate and to take turns. You need to choose activities that are suitable for your child as well as those that fit into your routine together.

In the following Table, the list of activities has been divided up into two levels—*early* and *advanced*. Early skills are appropriate for very young children who are less mobile and less able to control their movements. The progression from early to advanced skills is gradual. Only a small number of examples have been provided on these sheets. They will give you an indication of your child's level. You can add other items to these lists from the activities described later (see pp. 133–141).

Look at your activity lists when you have filled them in and see what your child was able to do.

Very few items ticked

If you have only a few items ticked, then you will need to concentrate on very simple activities to build up your child's skills of *attending* and *looking* at something with you. This skill needs to develop before you can expect him to start imitating things that you do, or taking turns with you. Simple suggestions have been listed under 'Looking together—early skills' (p. 134).

Two to three items ticked at the early level

If your child has two to three items ticked at the early level in any of the three basic skills, you would be wise to give him further practice by selecting activities from those listed under 'early skills' (pp. 134, 137 and 139). When you are confident that he can manage these, start selecting activities from the

Activity List—Preverbal skills

Child's name:................................. Date:..................................

1 LOOKING TOGETHER

	Did the child look with you?			Did the child look with you?	
Early skills	YES	NO	*Advanced skills*	YES	NO
a) Will the child look intently at your face when you put it close to his?			a) Will the child look when you sing a nursery rhyme with hand movements, e.g. 'Twinkle, twinkle little star'?		
b) Will the child watch while you move a toy from left to right in front of his line of vision?			b) Will the child look at pictures with you in a picture book or folder?		
c) Will the child look at a toy rattle when you shake it in front of him?			c) Will the child look when you rattle the cutlery drawer in the kitchen and suggest that he help take the items out?		
d) Will the child look at teddy when you are holding him and then look back at you?			d) Will the child look when you sit and 'talk' with a hand puppet?		
Other items which my child does			*Other items which my child does*		
e)			e)		
f)			f)		

2 IMITATION—Encourage the child to do what you do

Early skills	Did the child imitate you?		Advanced skills	Did the child imitate you?	
	YES	NO		YES	NO
a) Will the child pat his hands together when you pat yours together close to him?			a) Will the child brush his hair after watching you brush your hair or his? Hand him the brush.		
b) Will the child pat teddy after you do?			b) Will the child touch his head after watching you do it?		
c) Will the child bang two blocks together after watching you? Place the blocks in his hands.			c) Will the child put clothes pegs in a container after watching you do it?		
d) Will the child cover his face with his hands and play 'boo' after watching you?			d) Will the child kiss teddy good night during a game after watching you do it?		
Other items my child does			*Other items my child does*		
e)			e)		
f)			f)		

3 TAKING TURNS—Involve the child in games or activities that require taking turns. Encourage him to take his turn after you have had yours. Say 'your turn'—my turn'.

Early skills	Did the child take turns?		*Advanced skills*	Did the child take turns?	
	YES	NO		YES	NO
a) Will the child take turns with you shaking a rattle, if you hand it to him and when you place it on the table or floor?			a) Will the child take turns throwing a ball or bean bag into a bucket, and insist that you take a turn?		
b) Will the child take turns rolling a soft ball to you?			b) Tidying up toys, will the child take turns picking up a toy and putting it in the box?		
c) Will the child take turns putting a block on a block tower? Use large blocks that are easy to handle.			c) Will the child take turns using a cutter to make shapes out of dough? Does he vary his shapes according to what you do?		
d) Will the child take turns splashing water with his hands in the bath? Does he wait and watch you before taking a turn?			d) Will the child take turns on the swing with you or with other children?		
Other items my child does			*Other items my child does*		
e)			e)		
f)			f)		

'advanced skills' lists. Introduce new activities one at a time.

Some skills ticked at the advanced level
If your child can do some, but not all of the tasks listed at the advanced skills level, then continue working at this level in all three skill areas, by selecting from the activities suggested under 'advanced skills' (pp. 135, 137 and 139).

All or most tasks ticked at the advanced level
If your child managed all or most of the tasks listed at the advanced level, then you need to move on to the next stage. It is time to add *sounds* and perhaps some *words* to your games. Listen and see if he is making any sounds as he plays with you. The chances are high that he has begun to do this. Add a sound to your game and encourage any attempt that he makes to imitate it. In the final part of this section we shall give you more information on how to do this. (p. 142).

Summary—Assessing preverbal skills
1 Using the checklists, observe your child in a variety of situations and see how well he can:
   a) *look together* with you at something of interest;
   b) *imitate* your actions;
   c) *take turns* with you in simple activities.
2 Decide whether your child needs more practice—repeat your observations a number of times.
3 Choose appropriate activities to extend his skills, starting with those he can already do.
4 If he is ready, start adding sounds or words to your games.

GO

PLAY ACTIVITIES TO ENCOURAGE PREVERBAL SKILLS

The essential preverbal skills of looking together, imitation and turn-taking can be encouraged during both the course of your normal everyday activities and in your play-times with your child. If he is very young or is functioning at an immature level, then choose very simple 'games' and routines and concentrate on getting him to *look at things with you* before you try to get him to imitate or take turns. Examples of activities which you can use have been listed under the headings:

1 Looking together
2 Imitates simple actions
3 Taking turns

The activities have been divided into:

a) early skills
b) advanced skills

Sometimes an activity may involve aspects of all three skills together. This is appropriate except when a child is at a very early level and needs to practise early attending skills. Do not expect him to imitate or take turns. This will come later.

General points to be remembered

1 *Involve* the child in what you are doing and turn it into a game-like activity. Make it fun for both of you.
2 Give the child *time* to respond and *encourage* any response that he makes.
3 *Repeat* the games and activities as often as you like—but do not go on for too long at any one time. Stop if your child becomes bored or restless.
4 Do not persevere with an activity if the child is obviously reluctant or upset. There is nothing to be gained by forcing him to join in. Avoid confrontation.
5 If an activity is not very successful, choose another one. Try the unsuccessful one on another day—it might work better.
6 Pick a time when both you and the child are in the right

frame of mind or mood. If you are feeling under pressure the games are unlikely to be a success.

7   Remember—you cannot make a child join in but you can encourage him to want to, by making the things you do together fun.

The activities listed in the following pages have been selected from a range of routine situations that occur during the course of a normal day. You will be able to think of other activities and other situations which better suit your routines. Do not hesitate to try out new ideas of your own. As you will see, you can take any activity that your child does—even a simple one like banging on a table—and turn it into a game between you and him.

Looking together
Remember! Looking together is made easier for the child if you keep the following points in mind:
   a) *physical closeness is important*—have the child *close* to you when you are looking at something together.
   b) *Same angle of view*—This can sometimes be helpful although it is not essential.
   c) *Time to watch*—give the child plenty of time to look at the focus of your attention.
   d) *Time to explore*—give the child plenty of time to explore new things—by feeling and touching as well as looking.

Activities for early skills
Indoor play-time—Choose bright objects and toys that move or make a noise and are colourful, e.g. mobiles (bought or home-made), bells on a string, pop-up toys, rattles, pull-along toys, wind-up toys, spinning tops, trains or buses or trucks with people or animals that can go in the train or on to the bus.
   Colourful puppets or even ones made from an old sock that you can move and 'talk' will also attract the child's attention.

Nursery rhymes—Nursery rhymes and action songs can be sung wherever you happen to be at any time of the day, e.g. Round and round the garden', 'This little piggy went to market', 'Rock-a-bye-baby', 'Humpty Dumpty', 'Twinkle, twinkle, little star', 'Hickory, dickory dock'. These encourage the child to look at you or at the actions you are doing to them, e.g. tickling his feet.

Hat, glasses—You can attract your child's attention by wearing unusual hats, sun-glasses, etc. Encourage him to pull them off. He, too, can have a go at wearing them.

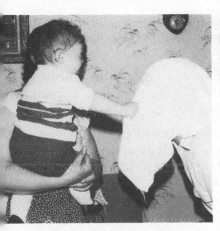

Bath-time—Hold floating or squeaky toys or a ball down under the water and let go of it suddenly. This is particularly effective if you have bubbles in the bath.

Bubbles—Blow bubbles for your child to burst. This activity is good practice in tracking objects.

Mirror—Look together at both yourself and your child in the wall mirror—wave and make faces. Later you could use a hand-mirror, such as a child's safety mirror.

Bed-time—Looking together at picture-books, photographs, etc., or soft toys such as teddy, and saying good-night as they are tucked into bed with the child. Kissing games, rubbing noses or blowing raspberries are also ways of saying 'sleep well'.

Activities for advanced skills
You can now begin to encourage your child to examine objects more closely. Here are some possibilities:

Getting dressed—Take him with you to the cupboard or drawer where his shirts and jumpers are kept. Take out three or four and let him help you choose which one he will wear today. Avoid confrontation by only offering acceptable choices.

Laying the table—Look together in the kitchen cupboard for the mugs or egg cups and let him help you put them in the right places on the table.

Picking flowers—Look together at the flowers in the garden. Smell the perfumed ones; let him help pick the ones you want for indoors.

Outdoor play-time—Water play—pouring, splashing, floating sticks, leaves or light toys. Sand play—digging, pouring, patting. Watching a balloon on a string.

Storytime—Looking at simple picture books together. Choose books with large, clear pictures of simple everyday objects and situations. Point out things of interest to the child; respond to the things that the child points out.
  Look at photographs of familiar people or objects, or pictures cut out of magazines and pasted onto card.

Going to the park or for a walk—Stop and look at a bird or a bee or a flower, or at a dog passing by. Look at the post box and the telephone box.

Going in the car—Look at the traffic lights and the buses and the people on bicycles.

Going shopping—In the supermarket, hand the objects you select to the child to look at and put in the basket. Smell the fruit. Do not try to do these things when you are in a hurry or feeling irritable!

Imitates simple actions
Remember! You can make imitating your actions easier for the child, if you keep the following points in mind:
  a) Start with actions you know your child can do, then gradually extend them.
  b) Make sure the child is *watching*. He will not be able to imitate you unless he sees what you are doing.

c) Encourage him to try by saying, 'You do it.'

d) If he is reluctant to try, *prompt* him. Move his hands gently to *show* him how to do the action.

e) Accept any attempts he makes during the early stages.

Activities for early skills
Nursery rhymes and action songs—Encourage the child to imitate your actions in games and songs, e.g. 'Do as I do', roly poly, touch parts of the face and body, clap hands, 'Here we go round the mulberry bush' etc.

Bed time—Pat teddy gently as you put him to bed and encourage your child to do the same. Kiss him good-night as well.

Indoor play-time—Play 'peek-a-boo' and encourage your child to hide his eyes with his hands.

Cover a toy or object with a cloth and say, 'Where's . . . ?' Remove cloth and say, '*There* it is!' Encourage your child to imitate the *actions* of covering and pulling the cloth off.

Getting up—If your child sleeps in a cot, put your hands up in the air and say, 'Up we get,' to encourage him to raise his arms. You can do this, too, at other times when you know he wants to be lifted up but is not raising his arms to indicate it.

Getting dressed—Have the child imitate your action of brushing or combing his hair.

Activities for advanced skills
From these beginnings you can move on to more advanced activities—even some that could be of help to you at home.

Indoor play-time—All sorts of games lend themselves to situations where imitating your actions is appropriate. It's important that you join in the games, even though you might feel embarrassed. How else can he imitate?

Playing with dolly or teddy—feeding, dressing and putting it to bed.

Kitchen play—cooking dinner, making tea, washing and putting away.

Playing with blocks—making towers, knocking them down, making trains and adding a chimney.

Playing with cars—pushing them under bridges, into garages, down ramps.

Musical instruments—bang drum, shake stick with bottle tops on.

Outdoor play-time—Sand play—dig, fill bucket, build castle, walk along a stick or beam. Climb through a tunnel. Climb up the steps of a climbing frame.

Storytime—Turning the pages of a book. Point to the picture.

Going shopping—Putting the objects in a bag or basket. Be sure that you leave some for the child to do.

Getting dressed—When dressing your child, say, 'What goes on next? That one!' and point to the shirt, socks or shoes if your child did not respond simultaneously. Encourage him to point before you put the item of clothing on.

Washing up—After eating, take the cutlery and dishes from the table and put them in the sink. Encourage your child to help you do this, taking one article at a time.

Cooking—Stir the ingredients in the mixing bowl and then offer the bowl to your child and let him stir.

When you are rolling the dough or patting it, give him a piece and encourage him to do what you are doing.

Washing clothes—Encourage him to take an item of clothing out of the laundry basket and put in in the machine. He may need a stool or to have you lift him up, but let him imitate your actions when you drop the clothes in the machine.

Workshop—Let him have a hammer and a piece of wood, just like yours. He may not mind that you have a nail and he has not.

Taking turns
Remember! You can make it easier for your child to learn to take turns if you keep the following points in mind:
  a) Choose an activity that will make your child *want* to join in.
  b) Make sure he is watching when you have your turn.
  c) Encourage him to take his turn by saying, 'Your turn'.

d) Encourage him to let *you* have *your* turn by saying, 'My turn', then 'your turn'.
e) Prompt him to take his turn, if necessary, by helping him to perform the appropriate action.
f) Praise him when he manages to do it by himself.

Activities for early skills
Indoor play-time—Take turns patting a suspended ball or mobile or bell, or rolling a soft ball backwards and forwards across the carpet or floor.

Tickling and giggling games—remember to let him tickle you.

Nursery rhymes and action songs—Action songs like 'Row, row, row your boat' and 'See-saw, Marjorie Daw' involve taking turns in leaning back and bending forwards. Also, let your child do the actions to you in 'Round and round the garden', 'This little piggy went to market', and so on.

Cuddles, squeezes and kissing games—You can take it in turns, particularly if you turn your face away so that your child has to make an extra effort to give you a kiss.

Balloons—Take it in turns to keep the balloon up in the air.

Echo!—Copy the babbling noises your child makes—you may be able to turn this into a conversation, even if you haven't a clue what you are talking about!

Push over—During your rough and tumble time, let your child push you over when you are down on all fours. When this game is well established (lots of laughter from your child), then take turns at pushing each other over.

Mirror—Take turns clapping hands in front of the mirror.

Bathtime—Take turns with the soap in the bath, or the scrubbing brush, or sprinkling the powder.

Activities for advanced skills
Once again, many everyday activities can help your child take turns, provided you give him the chance of joining in.

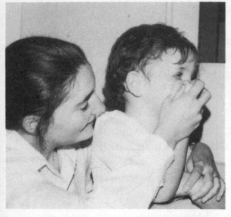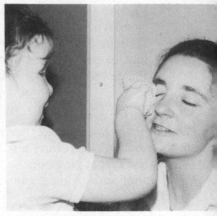

Washing up—You can take turns putting the knives, forks and spoons away—you do one, then let the child do one.

Cooking—Making dough, take turns stirring, rolling and cutting it.

Gardening—You can take turns with the small watering can—you water one pot and I'll water the next one!

Workshop—Take turns using the hammer—or picking up bolts or screws or nails that may have been spilt accidentally and need putting back in their containers.

Indoor play-time—Pushing a car backwards and forwards involves taking turns. So does throwing a bean bag and emptying the bucket. Picture lotto involves taking turns and can be played with more than just two people. Brothers and sisters often like to play, too.

Outdoor play-time—Take turns on the swing or on the slippery slide. Take turns using the shovel in the sand pit or the funnel in the water bucket.

Visiting friends or relations—Take turns knocking on the door—if you are visiting someone you know well, who does not mind having lots of knocks on the door.

Bed time—I'll take one step up the stairs—then you take one step—and we'll see how far we get before we are all out of order!

As you can see, the opportunities for joint activity are endless and, if you make the most of them, your child will soon be attending to things with you willingly, imitating what you do and trying to learn the things that are not so easy to imitate—particularly if you give him a little help and guide his movements when necessary, and then give him lots of chances to practice. He will learn to take turns both when you are playing games, like throwing a ball, or when you are doing 'real' things, like putting things away or cooking—which often seem like games anyway.

When you think your child is attending, imitating and taking turns readily, without a great deal of effort on your part any more, you can start concentrating on encouraging *sounds* and *words* with your games.

Summary—Everyday activities for preverbal skills

1   Choose activities from all the routine situations in the day.
2   Involve the child in what you are doing and make it fun.
3   Encourage any response you get from the child—but do not persevere if he gets upset or is not interested. Try another activity and go back to that one another day.
4   If your child cannot quite manage to do what you are doing, help him by showing him how and perhaps holding his hands while he makes the movement.
5   Give lots of opportunities—these skills need constant practice.
6   When the child is attending, imitating and taking turns often and easily, you can begin to concentrate on adding sounds to your game.
7   Remember, these skills are the foundation blocks for learning to use *language* and need a lot of practice.

PREVERBAL TO VERBAL COMMUNICATION—THE BEGINNING OF MEANINGFUL SOUNDS

In Section Two we noted that children often accompany their early gestures with a sound, but that the sounds are random; only gradually do they begin to use a *consistent* sound to indicate a particular person, object or activity. An early example of this may be 'dadadad' which the child makes as part of his repertoire of early sounds but which eager parents respond to by saying, 'Daddy!—yes, that's daddy!' So that, over a period of time, the child will come to associate this sound with a particular person. It may be that he will use 'dadad' to refer to Uncle Tom and the milkman as well, but gradually your reactions to this over-generalised use of the word will teach him that 'dadad' is only appropriate for one special person. He may learn the names of other members of the family, including the dog, in the same manner, and his early attempts may be far from perfect; but he will begin to use them *consistently*, so that both you and he know who he is talking about—'Nana' for granny, 'De-dee' for Daniel and 'Roof' for Rover.

This same process of beginning to use a particular sound to mean one specific thing, occurs with objects and activities as well as people. So 'brm-brm' may be used to refer to 'car'; 'boo' for a hiding game; 'whee' for the game you play with a ball and 'nish-nish' is his way of saying 'good-night'. Many of these early words are learnt as part of the early games you have been playing with him, as he has been learning to do things with you and take turns in all sorts of activities, so that his earliest use of 'brm-brm' may not mean the *object* 'car', but may refer to the *game* you play when you sit on the carpet and take turns pushing his red truck backwards and forwards, under the bridge and down the ramp. In the same way, 'whee' may be the word he uses when he wants you to play ball with him and 'bicky' will mean 'I want a biscuit, please'.

'Invented' words

Children's 'invented' words are an important stepping stone on the way to using real words. They include *expressive* and repetitive *sounds* that are easy to produce and are associated with activities and events important to the child. The sounds are often closely associated with the objects or actions that they represent. Two examples are 'tick-tock' for clock, and 'miaow' for cat, which are widely understood. They also include some *consistent sounds* which the child develops and uses to refer to specific objects and events before he has learnt the 'real' word. The most significant feature of these sounds is that each child will make up his *own* 'words' and they do not necessarily sound at all like 'real' words—but the important people in the child's life can usually work out what he is referring to because he will use the same 'word' every time he wants to refer to that specific object or event. Some examples are:

Expressive sounds	*Consistent sounds*
brum-brum—car	bicky—biscuit
whee—throw ball	da—that one
miaow—cat	wups—upstairs
tick-tock—clock	ta—thank you
boo—hiding game	tee-tee—teddy
oh-oh—all fall down	Nana—Granny *or* banana
yum-yum—nice to eat	boat—ice block
moo—cow	lala—apple
quack-quack—duck	far—vest
woof—dog	girp—get up

The use of invented words represents a significant step forward on the road towards being able to talk. From relying mostly on gesture accompanied by random sounds, the child is now using specific sounds to mean particular things—even if some of the sounds he is using are *immature* sounds (such as 'woof' and 'tick-tock') and some of the 'invented' words are part of a *private* language which only those who know the child well can understand. Most children who have reached this stage will make the transition from invented to conventional words quite easily. They will need to hear clear models of the conventional words used in as many situations as possible, but before they begin to use real words, it is very important to *accept* the immature form and continue to *encourage* the child to communicate in all his routine activities.

How can you help?
a) *Listen* to the sounds and 'invented' words that your child is

using. It may be helpful to make a tape-recording of a play session in which you and your child are involved in a routine activity or game with favourite and familiar objects. Play the recording back and listen to the sounds that accompany his repeated actions.
b) *Add* an expressive sound or word to your games.
c) *Which sound first?* Some sounds are harder for children to say early, so start with the easy ones.
d) What next—Add a word!

Listen to the sounds and 'invented' words that your child is using
Note down the sounds and invented words that your child uses during some of the routine activities and games that you are involved in daily. Tape-record some of these sessions and play them back afterwards. Make an appropriate sound as you perform the activity and encourage your child to imitate it.

Look at the list that Susan's mother has made, then *complete a list for your own child during the course of the next day or two.*

Susan has obviously begun to use consistent sounds for some of the important people, objects and actions in her daily routines. Her mother would be concerned to extend the range of situations in which she used expressive sounds and she would do this by deciding what word or sound to use and then encouraging Susan to use it as part of a game or daily activity, and making sure that all the other members of the family used the sounds and encouraged Susan, too.

Add an expressive sound to your games and activities
For many of the things that you do with your child, you may feel that an expressive sound is *inappropriate*. If you are talking about articles of clothing, or playing a game asking the child to touch his eyes, ears, nose, etc., you will prefer to use the *real* word, but accept whatever attempts the child makes when he begins to try and imitate you. His early attempts may result in 'invented' words which he will use consistently for quite some time before he learns to say the real word.

Yet again, there are other situations and games where an expressive sound is appropriate and more likely to be imitated than a real word in the early stages. Some real words can be

EXAMPLE—*List of expressive sounds and 'invented' words*

Child's Name: Susan   Date: 20th November

SOUND OR WORD	ACTIVITY
'uppy'	Getting up in the morning
'da' (that one)	Dressing—choosing clothes
'eggy'	Breakfast
'oh-oh' (something's fallen or broken)	In the kitchen
'oo' (spoon) 'bup' (cup)	Objects
'Vo-vo' (Rover, the dog) 'Nen' (sister Jennifer) 'Nana' (granny)	Names
'brum' (car) 'boo' (hiding game) 'whee' (throwing ball)	Play-time
'quack-quack' (duck) 'woof' (dog) 'miaow' (cat) 'oink-oink' (pig)	Story time
'ni-ni' (good night)	Bed time

made to sound like expressive sounds by over-emphasising them or adding an extra syllable. Some suggestions are listed below and you will think of many more words to add to the list.

Gardening
    dig-dig—digging in the flower bed
    p-u-l-l—pulling up weeds
    swish-swish—watering the flowers

List of expressive sounds and 'invented' words

Child's Name: .... Date: ....

SOUND OR WORD	ACTIVITY

Workshop
  bang-bang—hammering
  see-saw—sawing

Washing clothes
  in-you-go—putting clothes in washing machine or basket

Outdoor play-time
  splish-splash—pouring water
  pat-pat—patting sand

Going for a walk
  bzzz—bee
  tweet-tweet—bird
  woof—dog
  algone—posting a letter in the box

Bath time
  rub-a-dub-dub—drying with the towel
  bub-bub—bubbles
  scrub—scrubbing brush

Bed time
  ni-ni—good night
  sh!—putting teddy to bed

Rhythms and tunes
  row-row (Row your boat)
  wee (This little piggy)
  f-a-ll (Humpty Dumpty)

Play-time
  whee—as you throw the ball
  ssh—teddy to bed
  dring-dring—telephone

Many opportunities can be provided to give practice in a variety of situations, once a new sound has been added.

  —*Animal sounds* can be made looking at picture books, solving puzzles, playing with farmyard toys and singing songs, such as 'Old MacDonald had a farm'.
  —*Cars, trucks, buses* and trains can be played both inside and out and the sounds 'brum-brum', 'toot', 'choo-choo' can

be encouraged during games, when looking at pictures, or when you see the real objects on your outings.

—*Doll and teddy play* provides opportunities for feeding, washing and putting to bed and the sounds used in 'real' situations can be extended to these—'yum-yum' or 'mmmmm' when something nice is eaten, a 'humming' when you rock dolly to sleep, 'ff' for drinking and 'sh' when you put dolly to bed. These can be used again when you look at pictures of these common activities.

—*Block play*. 'Ah' when it gets very high and 'oh-oh' when it falls down, and blocks can also be transformed into trains and cars; 'in' when you are dropping blocks into a container.

—*'Gone box'*. Small objects or pictures can be 'posted' in a shoe-box or cardboard container that has a hole or flap cut in the lid. The sound can be made as the objects are posted—or as they are retrieved!

—*Action songs* provide excellent opportunities. Often it will be the key word only that is emphasised and this is the one the child will join in and say at first:

> This little piggy went to market
>   (wee, wee, wee)
> Round and round the garden
>   (tickly under *there*)
> Ring-a-ring-a-roses
>   (all fall *down*)
> *See-saw* Marjorie Daw
> *Row, row, row* your boat
> *Hickory, dickory dock*

Musical instruments can be 'real' or 'pretend'—accompanied by 'bang-bang', 'toot-toot', 'ting-a-ling' and many more!

Which sound first?

Some sounds are easier for children to say than others, so it is wise to choose sounds and words from those that children develop early and to add the other, more difficult sounds later. Listen, too, to the sounds that your child is using. When you come to choose words to add to your games, start with words that have a sound you know your child can make.

Early sounds: b, p, d, m, t, n, g, ng, (as in si*ng*), h
Later sounds: s, f, l, y (as in *y*ou), w, sh (*sh*ip), th, (*th*ing), ch
(*ch*ew)

What next?–add a word
Your child has come a long way from when his earliest
messages were sent using gesture and random sounds. His
gestures became more specific and so did his sounds. By taking
part in lots of routine activities and games with you, he learned
to look at things with you, to imitate your actions and to take
turns. He learned about objects and activities by interacting
with them through you and gradually started using sounds and
'invented' words with the actions in your routine games. He is
now ready to start learning 'real' words. You will have been
using 'real' words in some of your games, such as touching
parts of the body, or naming objects as you lay the table, or
when you are dressing or undressing the child. But in some of
your action games and when looking at books, you may have
been using expressive sounds, such as 'quack-quack, 'oh-oh'
and 'whee!' Now is the time to add the real word as well, said
simply and clearly as you push the car, or look at a picture of a
duck, or throw the ball.

So whatever activities or objects you are involved with, pair
a clear word with the object or action and the child will soon
associate the word with the object; it will not be long before he
begins to substitute the real word for his sounds. Section Five
will tell you more about encouraging first words.

Summary. The beginning of meaningful sounds
1   Before children start using real words, they use expressive
sounds and invented words. These are important stepping
stones on the path to learning to talk and should be encouraged
and extended.

2   When the child is using lots of expressive sounds and
'invented' words, it is time for you to provide him with the
'real' word. Say the real word clearly each time the object or
activity is appropriate and your child will gradually learn to say
it, too.

3   Choose words that are made up of easy sounds first.

Your child has now mastered the important preverbal skills of looking together, imitation and taking turns. He has begun to use consistent sounds with his actions and he is ready to learn the 'real' words for the many objects and activities that play such an important part in his daily life. He will need your help to take the next step—starting to use real words.

SECTION FIVE: THERE'S A WORD FOR IT

We can expect children to learn 'proper' words when they can do three things:

* Show they can *communicate* through gestures or by tone of voice.
* Show by their gestures, actions or their ability to follow what you say that they have the understandings necessary for words.
* Produce a *consistent sound pattern* linked to actions or gestures or, better still, copy another person's sounds.

> If your child *cannot* do these things, then you must keep working on him. See Sections Two, Three and Four. It is too soon to start on proper words.

> If your child can do these three things, or if he has some words already, then this section is for you. Read on. Also, many of the ideas in this section can be used with children who are learning a sign language, such as *Makaton* or *AmerInd*.

What you will read about in this section

ON YOUR MARKS

What is a word? The special thing about words is their *meaning*. This is more crucial then saying them correctly.

How children acquire words. A child learns the meaning of words not just by listening, but by being involved in activities with people, objects and events. This helps him puzzle out the link between the words he hears spoken and their meaning.

GET SET

Selecting words for your child to learn. We provide you with a special form, listing over 60 common words. This will help you to pinpoint all the words your child knows or says, as well as the most likely new words for him or her to learn. Our recommendation is that you concentrate on five to ten new words for a month at a time, although your child's pace will guide you here.

GO

Learning new words. We describe three steps children take in learning new words and what you can do to help at each step.

Step 1: Grasping the *meaning.*

Step 2: Child *chooses to imitate* the word.

Step 3: Child *thinks* of the word without help.

We give examples of how five different words could be taught in everyday situations and provide guidelines which you could use to help your child master the new words you have chosen.

Finally, we describe ways of reviewing progress at the end of every month and after every six months. These reviews will help you to decide on more new words for the child to learn and whether the time has come to move on to the next stage of language development—talking in sentences.

ON YOUR MARKS

WHAT IS A WORD?

The Germans call it *Klosett*, but in Yugoslavia it is known as *Nuznik*; the Italians talk about *gabinetti*, while in Ireland it is referred to as *leithreas*. All very different words, yet each refers to the same thing. In fact, there must be thousands of words, given the number of languages used in the world. In most cases, there is no good reason why one combination of sounds was chosen for the name of any particular thing, rather than another. Each society or tribe invented its own words which became a private code known only to them and not to outsiders.

These words—the creations of our ancestors—have two key features which are as real today as they were at the birth of the word.

* Everyone in the tribe agreed to use the same sound or combination of sounds. *The word was agreed.*
* Even more important, everyone used the word to refer to the same thing, or persons or places or events. *The meaning was agreed.*

Every known language has a system of sounds linked with a system of meanings and hence every tribe had to teach its young not only the words to speak, but also what each word meant.

Inventing new languages

The power of our ancestors to create languages can still be ours today. Writers of fiction like Jonathan Swift in *Gulliver's Travels* or George Orwell in his novel *1984*, have done it. Rather more ambitious was the attempt made by Ludwik Zamenhof to create an international language—Esperanto—that could be readily learnt by all peoples of the world and thus translate the hope of world peace into reality, through nations communicating more easily with one another. Sad to say, his creation has not been a stunning success. But then the number of people who can speak two or more languages fluently is not all that high, either. A tribute, some would say, to the power our mother tongue has over us.

It is very much easier for people to create new words in their own language. Among the recent inventions in English are 'wets' (attributed to Margaret Thatcher) and 'Reaganomics' (guess who). Nor is this just another privilege of the famous. Everyone can do it and most do, especially young children. For instance, one girl, Jane, when she first started to talk, christened one of her uncles 'Joleo', and for a time this became his name within the family (previously he was called 'Gerald'). Other children invent their own names for favourite objects or activities.

Can you think of any examples from your family or even words you invented as a child?

THE WORD	ITS MEANING

I suspect the actual sounds or words you have written in the left-hand column bear little resemblance to the proper English words. But of course, that did not matter at the time. The crucial thing was that all the family got to know the meaning of the invented word. Then they could start to use it in their daily conversations.

> Any sound or sounds can become a word as long as everyone understands its meaning.

There comes a time, however, when children and families stop using their private words and revert to the proper ones. Generally this occurs when the toddler comes into contact with more people outside the family—babysitters, neighbours, playmates or playgroup leaders. These people cannot be expected to know—or remember—each infant's collection of private words. Instead they encourage the children to use the conventional words. How? By their failure to understand when the children come out with their own words. They can even be heard to say, 'I don't know what you mean.' This breakdown in communication is the starting point of a process that will force a child to master the proper words of his native language.

HOW CHILDREN ACQUIRE WORDS

It is so long since you experienced this that I am sure you have forgotten the problems children face. In fact you are much more likely to see it only from an adult's perspective.

For instance, take those four foreign words I used at the beginning of the chapter. How could you find out what they mean?

The most common answer is to look them up in a dictionary or ask a person who knows Irish, Italian, etc. We shall save you the trouble of doing either and tell you that they all mean *toilet*.

Straight away you have picked up the meaning of these

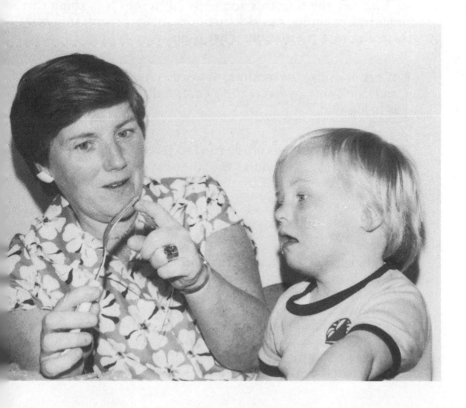

foreign words. But you did it by a process of translation—a process that children cannot possibly use. To be able to understand the translation, you must already know one language. An example with a child might make this clearer.

CHILD: (picking up a fork) Spoon.
ADULT: (watching) That's not a spoon. It's a fork. See all the sharp-pointed bits it has for sticking into your food.

Everything the adult says makes perfect sense—provided you already know English. But remember, this child probably knows only a handful of words. How can he or she possibly cope with the 20—yes 20 words (count them and see)—spoken by the adult; including words like 'not', 'pointed', 'sticking'. In fact, the child would be hard-pushed even to recognise which one of the 20 is the name of an eating utensil with sharp-pointed bits.

You see, the trap this adult has fallen into is to think that infants, like adults, can pick up the meaning of words simply by listening to a translation. That is not so.

> When learning the meaning of words, children have to look and think about what is going on, as well as listening to what is being said.

How, then, would you have tried to teach the child the word 'fork'? What might you as the adult have done?

1.
2.
3.
4.

Among the ideas we ourselves listed were: a) say one word—'fork'—as child holds and examines the fork; b) let him or her handle it and feel the points; c) have the child use a fork when eating; d) as the child examines the fork, say its name; e) show the child other sorts of forks—big/small, plastic/metal— or pictures of forks, so that he realises that 'forks' come in all shapes and sizes.

You may have listed extra ways of helping, but I am sure

your methods, like ours, involve the child in looking at or experiencing the object you are naming.

> Words only become meaningful to the child when he can link them to an experience or sensation.

This is such an important point that we will repeat it over and over in this section. Remember, mere listening is *not* sufficient to learn the meaning of words—children have to use their other senses as well.

Problems with words

There are two other difficulties that children are likely to encounter with words, only this time the fault—if that is the correct word—lies with the language.

First, we have different names for the same thing. Take 'toilet', for instance. It is also called lavatory, bathroom, WC, ladies or gents, loo . . . can you think of others? To use different words could confuse children, especially those who are slow learners. All the adults in the child's life must agree to stick to the same word in the early stages.

The second problem is that there are many different words referring to various parts of the same object. We can hold up a fork in front of the child and say, 'fork' or, 'it's silver', or 'metal', 'eating with', 'it's mine', 'it's yours', etc., etc. Once again, the child is in a dilemma. Are these different names for the same thing—like loo, bathroom, WC for toilet? If not, what do all these new words mean???

You must beware of flooding the child with too many words. Stick to one word per object or event at a time. Indeed, that is why starting with names of people is such a good idea—every person has one name.

Once the child knows the meaning of a word—e.g. 'fork'—then you can introduce some of the other meanings associated with that object: 'sharp', 'prongs', 'silver'.

First words

Which words do children generally learn first? We have listed them on our FIRST WORDS form (p. 159). As you can see, we have grouped the words into five categories.

1 *Names of people*—You will have to write in the family names or names given to pets or favourite soft toys. These differ from family to family. The important feature of these words is that they refer to *one* person or plaything in the child's life.

2 *Names of objects*—This list could have gone on and on. We have kept it short but left room to add in other words, particularly objects which your child likes or ones found in your home.

3 *Social words*—As you read down this column, you will see that these are the words used when we are being sociable—'bye', 'hello', or to communicate a basic idea—yes, no, 'what' (for 'what's that'), or 'look' (plus pointing).

4 *Action words*—This is a different set of words again. These refer to events performed either by people or objects. As you see, most of the words, but not all, are verbs. Children sometimes use other words to describe actions, e.g. 'in' for 'put in' or 'down' for 'fall down' or 'up' for 'lift up'. Notice, too, that the words *brush* and *comb* also feature in this column. As well as being the names of objects, these same words are used when talking about the action of brushing or combing.

5 *Modifiers*—These are words which further describe objects or people. They tell you more abut them—big/dirty/nice. Sometimes the words are not so descriptive—'that', 'this', 'my', 'your'. Yet even these words serve to single out one object from the others.

How were the words chosen?
The sixty or so words listed on the form were chosen in three ways.

* First, these were the words young children—both handi-capped and non-handicapped—were observed to learn first. Various researchers have monitored children's language development and so, for a few children at least, we know precisely the first words they learned and the order in which they acquired them.

* Second, we picked words that refer to objects and events

FIRST WORDS FORM

Child's Name: ....

Date started: ....

People		Objects		Social		Actions		Modifiers	
	Spon Imit		Spon Imit		Spon Imit		Spon Imit		Spon Imit
Mummy		Ball		Bye		Brush/Comb ..		Big	
Daddy		Book		Gimme		Down		Bold	
		Car		Hello ⌐		Drink............		Clean	
Child's Name		Chair		Hiya ⌐		Eat		Dirty	
Other names		Comb		Here		Fall (down) ...		Hot	
		Cup		Look............		Go		Little/Small ...	
		Dinner		Nite-nite.........		Gone/All gone		More............	
		Doll		No		In		My	
		Milk............		There............		Kiss		Nice	
		Shoe		What............		Off		Sick	
		Spoon		Where		On		That	
		Sweet		Yes		Sit (down) ...		This	
		Teddy............				Sleep		Your	
PRONOUNS				(Toilet)		Stop............			
Me						Throw			
Mine						Up			
I						Want			
You						Wash			
It									

that frequently occur in a young child's environment. These are *useful* words because the children can communicate their needs and wants through them.

* From our work with families of children having difficulty learning language, we have identified the words they find easier to pick up or ones which are relatively easy to teach.

Why the five categories?

We had two reasons for grouping the words into categories:
* First, children generally find it easier to learn certain types of words. Names of people are easiest; then come either names of objects or social words depending, it would appear, on what the family chooses to focus on, and then action words, modifying words and pronouns.

In our experience, it is a good idea to work from left to right on the First Words form when it comes to selecting words for your own child to learn. We hasten to add, however, that we are talking generally. Some children's first words can be modifiers like the words 'bold' or 'naughty'.

* Our second reason is with an eye to the future. As you will read in Section Six, when children come to join words into sentences, they do it in a regular and consistent way. It is not done haphazardly. Very often they link one type of word with another, e.g. a social word plus name of person to give sentences like, 'Hello, Mummy', 'Bye, Paul', 'No, Paul', 'Look, Mummy' (p. 181 gives you further details)

It is important, therefore, that children know words from all five categories, so that they can construct a full range of sentences.

> It is better for children to know 20 words from five different categories than 20 names all from the same category.

We shall now describe how you can use the form to help your child learn new words.

GET SET

SELECTING WORDS FOR YOUR CHILD TO LEARN
Your selection will depend on:
* the words your child already says;
* the word your child *needs* to know;
* the words your child is ready to learn.

You will discover the answers as you work through the activities in this section.

Activity 1: Adapting the First Words form for your child
Look back at the *First Words* form. We deliberately left blank spaces under each column so that you could write in words that *your child* needs to know. You should now write in on the form:
* The names of the people in your family with whom the child has *frequent* contact —brothers and sisters, 'granny', 'uncle', etc. But do not put down too many names, only the really key people.
* The names of any favourite toys or objects, for instance, 'teaser' (the child loved Maltesers) or 'blanket' (her favourite comforter) or 'pans' (playthings).
* The word your family uses for the toilet—'wee-wees', 'potty', etc.
* Any other words that you feel it is important for your child to know and use.

Activity 2 : The words your child already knows and uses
You can use the form to pinpoint all the words your child uses, even if it is only in imitation of you. First we shall describe what counts as a word and then tell you how to use the form.

What's a word?—The following count as words for this activity:
1 The words we listed on the form, spoken sufficiently clearly for nearly everyone in the family to understand what the child says. (The child can change them slightly, e.g. 'mama' for 'mummy', or 'hi' for 'hello', etc.)
2 'Babyish' words but ones that everyone is likely to know, e.g. child says 'woof, woof' for dog.

3   Child's 'invented' words but said consistently and clearly enough for the meaning to be understood by the family. For instance, 'Den-Den' for Denis (child's brother), 'la-la' (one boy's word for apple), 'at-fat' (a girl's word for going outside).

On the form you should:

1   Write in the sound or word the child actually uses (see sample form, p. 163).

Note: If the meaning of your child's word is already listed on the form, put your child's word in brackets beside it. If it is a new meaning, write the word in the spaces provided.

2   Tick the appropriate column as follows:

—if the child thinks of the word himself, that is, uses the word *spontaneously*, then tick the *'spon'* column.

—if the child can copy you saying the word, that is, the adult says the word immediately before the child, then tick the column headed *'Imit'* (for imitation).

(Note: Do this if the adult has used the word in a sentence, e.g. Adult: 'Give the ball to me'—Child: 'Ball'.)

3   Put the words into their appropriate categories. Generally this will be obvious, but some words can refer to an action as well as the name of the object—brush, comb, bath, etc. You will have to decide by observing what was happening whether your child was talking about the object or the action. If you are not sure where to put a word, make a guess. This is your list and you know best what your child meant!

What words is your child ready to learn?

Do not be too disheartened if your child has few or no words recorded on the form; we have not finished yet.

As well as saying words, children have to know their meanings. In fact, this understanding must come before speech. You can also use the form to identify the words your child understands. For this, you should think of it as a listing of *meanings* and we want you to circle those meanings your child knows.

Your child can show he knows the meaning of a word in three ways:

Sample

Child's name: Rory ....   FIRST WORDS FORM   Date started: 6th June ....

People

	Spon	Imit
Mummy	✓	
(Daddy)	✓	
Child's Name		
Other names		
Paul	✓	
(Mary)		
PRONOUNS		
Me		
Mine		
I		
You		
It		

Objects

	Spon	Imit
Ball	✓	
(Book)		✓
(Car)		✓
Chair		
Comb		
Cup		✓
Dinner		
Doll	✓	
Milk		
Shoe (ooey)		
Spoon		
Sweet	✓	
Teddy	✓	
Tea		
(dog)		

Social

	Spon	Imit
(Bye)		
Gimme		
Hello		
Hiya		
Here	✓	
Look		
Nite-nite		
(No)	✓	
There		
What		✓
Where		
Yes	✓	
Potty (Toilet)		
Please		

Actions

	Spon	Imit
Brush/Comb		
Down		
Drink		✓
Eat		
Fall (down)		
Go		
(Gone) All gone		
(In)		
Kiss		
Off		
On		
Sit (down)		
Sleep		
Stop		
Throw		
(Up)		
Want		
Wash		

Modifiers

	Spon	Imit
Big		
Bold		
Clean		
Dirty		
Hot		
Little/Small		
More		
My		
Nice		
Sick		
That		
This		
Your		

a) By the *gestures* used. For example, wave of hand to indicate *Bye-bye*, raised hand to be lifted *up* or shake of head for *no*.

b) By the *actions* performed. In play, the children may pretend to give a doll *drink* or put it to bed (*sleep*) or they may place objects inside (*in*) or on top of another (*on*).

c) By *understanding* what you say. For example, you say 'Where's Paul?' and the child looks round to see Paul, or you say, 'Give teddy a kiss', and he does, suggesting that he can understand the meaning of 'kiss'. Beware, though. The child may not be understanding your words at all—it merely looks that way. For instance, you say, 'Put the toys in the box', and the child does. He appears to obey you, but equally, had you said nothing, he might have started to put the toys in the box anyway because it is something he likes doing. Or you might even have said 'Box in the put toys the', and the child would still have obeyed! because he knows that is what you do before bath-time each day.

Go through the form, circling the meanings that you are sure your child knows. Remember to write in those that you have observed but which are not listed.

Collecting the information
Here are some tips to bear in mind when collecting the information needed for this form.

1 *Be strict.* Only record the words or meanings you have actually heard or seen your child use on a *number of occasions* recently. This is vital when it comes to the stage of selecting new words.

2 *Consult others.* Make a copy of the form so that you can pin it up in the kitchen or living-room. You can easily add new information as it comes. Discuss the form with everyone in the house. Have they heard your child use other words?

   If your child attends playgroup or school, talk to the leaders about the words they have heard your child use.

3 *Observing.* Over a period of several days, write down on a plain sheet of paper all the gestures, sounds or words which you notice your child using to communicate. The whole family can help to make this as comprehensive as possible. This information can be transferred later to the First

Words form. This activity is especially recommended if your child does not seem to understand or to use many words.

4   *Listening.* For children who have begun to use words, we suggest you try the following:
Tape record yourself and your child during a favourite activity, e.g. playing with teddy or looking at a book. Around ten minutes is usually enough. Afterwards, replay the tape, writing out all the words the child said but paying special attention to unclear but persistent sounds he used. If you listen to these a number of times, you may discover what your child meant. For example, one girl said 'gup', which we later realised meant *get up*. Another child, when putting dolly to bed, repeated a word that sometimes sounded like 'nite', at other times like 'nice' and occasionally it could be heard as 'now'. It is likely the adults she played with used all three words 'night, dolly' 'that's nice' . . . 'now' . . . but the child merged them into one word.

You may discover your child is actually saying more than you thought.

This activity, especially if repeated by others in the family, can be a real ear-opener!

Summary

* On the *First Words* form tick the words you are sure your child uses and circle the meanings he or she understands.

* For several days, keep a list of all the words/sounds/gestures your child uses to communicate. Involve all the family in this.

* Tape record a ten-minute play session when your child is likely to be talkative. As you replay the tape, list all the words or consistent sounds your child uses. Repeat this several times.

* Update the First Words form with the information obtained.

GO

LEARNING NEW WORDS

With so many new words to learn, it is very easy to feel lost or even despairing. Hence, our first bit of advice is:

Select a small number of words—say between five and ten

This means that you (and the family) can easily remember the new words you want your child to learn. It gives sufficient variety for teaching and increases the likelihood that your child will catch on to some, if not all of them. You can include different sorts of words within your selection.

The problem now is: Which words do I pick? The *First Words* form will guide you.

1 Look for words that you have circled on the form. Remember that these are the ones whose meaning you feel the child knows. Write these below:

My child seems to know these meanings:

2 Have you heard the child imitate any of these words or use a sound that is like the proper word? Rewrite the above words in the appropriate column:

Words imitated	Sounds like a word

3   Now read down the two lists above and circle those words which you feel would be most useful for your child. For example, it would help him get what he wants and thus cut down on frustration.

You may not need to go through all these three steps. You may have discovered your target words in the very first step, but it is a bonus if the child says a sound that is close to the proper word (Step 2).

4   Finally you have to decide on the *actual* word you want your child to learn. Sometimes you have a choice—woof-woof, doggie or dog. Pick one and everyone in the family should stick to it.

We are often asked if baby-words such as gee-gee and woof-woof should be encouraged. If your child finds them easier to say than the proper word then use them, but if they are no easier you might as well start with the proper name.

5   Now you can write down the target words you are going to concentrate on for the next month. A copy of the chart should be pinned up at home for all the family to see. Later you can write in the activities you will use to teach the words.

NEW WORDS FOR	(month)
	ACTIVITY

Steps in learning new words
There are three steps every child goes through when learning new words.

STEP 1 : GRASPING THE MEANING

What the child has to do

1   Understand the meaning of the word—best done by experience, such as being actively involved in a variety of contexts.
2   Link the word he hears spoken by the adult to its meaning.

What the adult can do to help

1   Highlight the meaning of the word to the child by showing it in a variety of contexts.
2   Say the word clearly and repeat it so that the child can learn it and link it to its meaning.
3   Use the same word; do not introduce others that have similar meanings, e.g. toilet, wee-wee, bathroom, loo, etc.

Remember: In this stage, **the child need not talk**. Rather, your efforts should be directed at getting him actively participating. Be warned, this stage can take some time. The child has a lot of thinking to do.

STEP 2: CHILD CHOOSES TO IMITATE THE WORD

What the child has to do

Of his own accord, the child *chooses* to copy you during the activity. The initiative must come from him, but your response is crucial.

What the adult can do to help

1   Give the child time to come out with the words. During the activity, do not talk too much and be prepared to wait. One boy regularly took ten seconds before he copied his dad saying the new word.
2   The child's attempt at saying the word may not be very good to begin with, but it is a start. Tell the child he is right, repeat the word, smile, clap hands—anything that lets him know he has done something really good.

Remember: The child needs lots of practice at this stage before you move on to the next. You must continue saying the word. The most common mistake we find is that parents move on too quickly to Step 3. **Take your time.**

STEP 3: CHILD THINKS OF THE WORD WITHOUT HELP

What the child has to do

1   The child has to think about what he wants to say, i.e. the *meaning* he wants to convey.

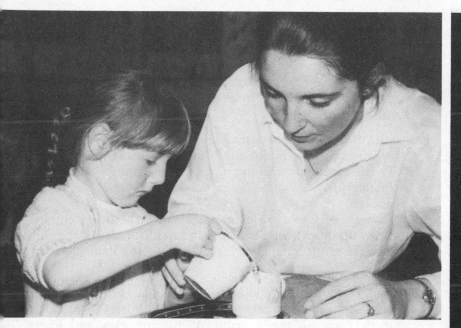

2 The child has to remember the word for this meaning.
3 The child has to remember how to speak this word.
What the adult can do to help
1 Keep the same activity going, so that the child has time to think. Do not switch too quickly to other activities.
2 Give the child some clues to help him remember, such as saying the first sound in the word 'f . . . all' or a linking word 'all . . . fall down'.
3 Accept your child's attempts—they may be the best he or she can do. Usually these are more indistinct than when he is imitating you. Through time, and with your examples, he will improve.

Remember: Even when children start to think of the words by themselves, they still need to practise. Keep on with the activities the child enjoys. Do not move on too soon to new activities and new words.

To summarise, then, adults can help children master new words with *V. R. M.*—not a new wonder drug, merely,
   V Variety of activities that children can actively join in.

R   *Reiterating* or *repeating* the word.
M   *Making* the *meaning* of the word clear.

Everyday contexts

Now for some examples of these rules in practice. We have taken one or two words from each column of the *First Words* form.

FAMILY NAMES (Brothers/sisters)
  Meal-times—Going round the table, pointing everyone out.
  People coming in and out of rooms—Naming them.
  Photograph Albums—Naming the 'key' people in the photos.
  Play-time—Child on mum/dad's knee; the other children crawl up quickly one at a time and tickle or nuzzle the child (should result in laughter). Adult says: 'It's Paul . . . Joan', etc.

NAMES OF OBJECTS (We have chosen parts of the body: 'Ear'—useful if child gets sore ears—and 'knees')
  Bath Time—Make a point of naming ears and knees, preferably as the child washes himself—or you! The same applies when drying.
  Car Journeys—If the child is on your knee, you can easily talk about ears and knees. Laugh, giggle as the child touches your ears and knees and say the words, 'Oh, my knees!'
  Songs—You can make up songs or use ready-made ones which repeat the words and link them with an action. 'These are my ears . . . here are my ears' (as you tug ears).
  Photographs or Posters—While looking at these, you can pretend to wash, dry, poke or tickle the person's ears and knees!

SOCIAL WORDS ('Gimme!'—A very important word!)
  Washing dishes—Child is allowed to take a turn at washing the dishes (plastic ones recommended) in the sink. But the washer has a helper who passes the dishes over. Initially, the child passes as you say 'Gimme'. Then when it is the child's turn to wash, you pass over the dishes, modelling the word 'Gimme' or 'Give-me' as you do.
  Those with dishwashers can still use the word when you are

loading and unloading the dishes and stacking them on the table.

(The child's earliest attempts will probably sound like 'Gimme', but later he will come to use the more correct version. It is wise to be patient.)

Mealtimes—Passing foodstuffs around the table—'Gimme milk . . . salt . . . sugar, etc.' (At this early stage do not worry about the lack of 'please' and 'thank you'. They, too, will come in time.)

Play-time—Choose a toy that has a number of different parts to it, e.g. building blocks, formboards or rings on to stacks. 'Gimme' can be linked to the child's requests for another piece.

Shopping—The child can hand you things when shopping in the supermarket. Point to what you want, saying 'give me', When you get home, let the child put the things away in the cupboard. Now he or she has a turn to say 'Gimme' before getting the objects to put away.

ACTION WORDS ('Up')

Generally—Use the word whenever the child wants to be lifted up or when you lift him or her up. You can also say it as you both go upstairs.

Play-time—In rough and tumble games, when you swing the child around, etc., break off the game and sit or lie down. As the child tries to pull you up, say 'up'. Repeat as long as you have the energy.

Walks—When out for a walk, lift the child up so that he can see over walls, reach trees, see shop windows, etc. Say 'up' as you do it.

Playground—A great place for learning action words. 'Up' occurs best with slides and climbing frames.

Bringing in the washing—Lift the child up to take the clothes off the line; let him down as he puts them *in* the basket and then lift again. Exhausting for you but lots of chances to learn the word 'up'.

MODIFYING WORDS ('Dirty')

Washing clothes—As the child puts the dirty clothes into the sink or washing machine, say 'dirty' to each. Also works well at dish-washing time when there are really dirty dishes!

Dolls—Plastic dolls can be specially dirtied with coal dust or mud for this game. Before the child washes the doll, emphasise how dirty it is.

Dusting—Give the child (and dad) a duster as they go around polishing the furniture. Lots of scope for talking about 'dirty'.

Pictures in old magazines—Let the child 'dirty' the faces, clothes, etc. with soft pencil scribbles. Again, lots of scope for talking about dirty.

Get the idea?

Notice what we have done? First, we took an everyday activity that the child could join in. Second, we selected a feature of it to highlight the meaning of the new word we wanted the child to learn.

Third, there was plenty of repetition within the activity, so that the child had lots of chances to link the word with its meaning.

Lastly, we identified up to four different activities in which the word occurred. This not only gave the child plenty of repetition but showed him that the words mean the same, no matter what the context.

Activity

You should now be able to think of activities for each of the words you have chosen for your child.
Here are some ideas for tackling this task.
1   Two heads are better then one. Talk it over with the family or other parents.
2   List all the activities your child is involved in or likes to be involved in with mum and dad, or with brothers and sisters. Tick the following, but there must be others which your child particularly likes.

Bathtime	Hammering	Setting the table	Hiding games
Washing dishes	Shopping	Clearing the table	*Others*
Washing clothes	Walks	Brushing	....
Ironing	Playground	Playing with toys	
Watching TV	Looking at books	Rooting in cup-	....
		boards/drawers	....
Cutting grass	Car journeys	Emptying hand-	
		bags	....
Digging	Dusting/Polishing	Playing around	....

Do any of these activities lend themselves to the words you want your child to learn? Look back to the list you made on p. 167 and note down against each word at least one activity in which you could use that word often. We recommend only one word for each activity. If you have two or more words in the activity, the child might get the meanings of the words mixed up. Once the child has mastered one new word, you might then use that activity to teach another word.
3   Give any new activity a fair try. Children frequently may not take to it straight away—they may appear afraid of the unfamiliar. Or they may behave in a way you do not want. Let them have their way to begin with, but show them that your way is more fun. If things are not going too well initially, keep it short. Try again another day. We recommend three or four attempts before you give up on any activity.

4   Be prepared to switch activities to suit your objectives. For instance, one dad chose 'Give me' when washing dishes but switched to 'wash' when the child started to imitate him spontaneously. Be an opportunist and follow your child's lead.

Pitfalls

Here are three common pitfalls that await you. Make sure you do not make these mistakes.

Same word—different meanings. Some of our common words have very different meanings. For example, 'off' can be used to refer to 'out', as in 'lights out'; or 'take off', as in undressing; or 'fall off' when an object falls off a table. These three meanings are quite distinct. It will only confuse the child if you use these three activities to help the child learn 'off'. Rather you need three or four activities that mean 'lights off' *or* 'clothes off'. Pick one meaning only.

Same meaning—different words. The opposite can also arise. For example, the word for asking could be 'want', 'please', 'give me' or just 'me'. You have to pick one of these and stick to it. We recommend you choose the most obvious—'give me' or 'gimme'.

You must beware of confusing the child. We recall one mother who had taught her child 'bye bye' by having the child put his toys into the box. When she later came to teach the word 'in', she used a similar activity and wondered why Christopher kept saying 'bye bye' instead of 'in'. You know, don't you?

Child already has a word. You may discover that a child has invented his own word for what you are teaching or prefers to use another form, e.g. a baby form. We suggest you accept these words for the time being. The proper words can come later.

More new words

Each month we suggest you update your target listing of new words.

* Delete from the list the words your child has mastered (see

example). Remember to add the words he has learnt to the *First Words* form).
* Delete words that are proving too difficult or uninteresting for your child. You might come back to them later but do not make life miserable for yourself or your child.
* Keep on the chart the words your child has not picked up but which you feel are important for him or her to grasp.
* Add new words that you feel are worth including. You can decide on these in the same way as before. (see p. 166), but bear the following points in mind:
1 The form lists words that are generally useful for children to learn, but there may be others that would be especially suitable for your child, either because they reflect his interests—such as a favourite toy, activity or foodstuff—or because they refer to significant people or events in his life.

TARGET LISTINGS OF NEW WORDS

NEW WORDS FOR OCTOBER	
no	(Keep)
shoe	✓ learnt
milk	✓ learnt
book	(drop)
bus	✓ learnt
bath	✓ learnt
in	(drop)
please	(drop)
out	(Keep)

NEW WORDS FOR NOVEMBER	
no	
out	(want to go out)
over	(turn page over in book)
give-me	
wash	(likes bath)
hair	
splash	
kick	

2 Select your words from a category that has relatively few words ticked. If the child knows 15 names of objects but only one action word, then it is better to select one or two new action words than a 16th object name.
3 However, some categories of words are harder than others. Generally, the order of difficulty is:

Easiest   Names of people
           Names of objects/social words
           Actions
           Modifiers
Harder   Pronouns

Hence action words are best taught before modifiers and social words before action words, etc.

4 When you do come to modifying words, it is best to pick only one of the two *contrasts*, e.g. 'dirty' or 'clean' but not both. When the child has fully grasped the meaning of one, you can introduce the opposite.

If you want to succeed,

> Select words that reflect your child's interests and needs.

> DO NOT EXCEED TEN NEW WORDS AT A TIME

Every three months (or sooner), you should review your updated *First Words* form. This will help to keep you on course and let you spot whether your child is falling behind with one type of word. You could take action accordingly.

However, our prime reason for suggesting you do this, is for the encouragement it should give you. When children's progress is slow, it is all too easy to assume that they are no more advanced than they were six months ago. Frequently this is not the case.

We suggest you keep a monthly 'new words' list until you have recorded some 60 words or more that your child is using *spontaneously* on the *First Words* form, over all five categories. At this point he will have a basic vocabulary of words that should continue to grow as you play and interact with him.

However, you can now afford to devote your energies to helping him learn to join words into sentences, which is the theme of the next section.

Finally, a reminder of the main points you must remember if you are to prove successful:

* Pick words that the child already *understands*.

* Draw up a list of words (ten at the most) that it would be *useful* for your child to say.

* Think of a number of activities where those words occur often.

* As your child takes part in the activity, clearly link the new words with their meaning, e.g. saying 'wash' as he washes his hands.

* The child may need many opportunities before he attempts to use the words. Do not force him to copy what you say. Be content if he joins in the activity.

* Remember to accept any attempt by the child to say the new words. As the child practises them, his speech should become clearer.

* Keep the teaching activities short. Do not expect the child to learn if he is bored or tired. Several short sessions at different times are far better than one long one.

* If the child does not attempt to use a word after a week or so you may need to drop it and select another word to teach.

* When the child starts to use the new words, continue to give him practice at saying them, especially in new activities, and keep using them when you have moved on to teach other new words. This ensures that they become part of his everyday language.

SECTION SIX : MAKING SENSE OF SENTENCES

It is not enough for children to know lots of single words. To make good sense they must join their words into sentences. But as you will discover in this section, words do not go together in just any order. Children have to learn the *rules* for combining words. This is called the grammar or syntax of their language. Not surprisingly, they start simply—just two words at a time—but later their sentences will get longer as they master the rules.

This section is for you if your child:
* knows and regularly uses 30 or more words from at least three categories on the *First Words* form;
* has already started to put words together in short sentences, such as, 'bye, daddy', 'more bread', 'go away doggie';
* regularly talks in short sentences but leaves out the little words, like 'the', 'is', or gets confused about adding 's' or 'ed' to words.

If your child has not managed to get this far, you should continue with the ideas given in the earlier sections, but do read pp. 181-7 in this section, to get a better idea of what lies ahead of you. It may not be too long before your child starts to make sense through sentences.

What you will read about in this section

ON YOUR MARKS

Basic sentences rules. In order to convey his meaning exactly, a child must learn how to join words together correctly into sentences. Here we show you how to find out if your child is ready to start talking in sentences. He should be able to put two words together, should have a vocabulary of more than 30 words taken from at least three categories on the *First Words* form, should show some understanding of relationships and will have started imitating adult sentences. This foundation is essential if he is to go on to Phase One of sentence learning. We include tests to help you assess the stage he has reached.

GET SET

Monitoring your child's progress. We provide you with a special chart for recording your child's sentences and explain how to assess the results and decide whether he should progess to *Phase 1: Early Sentences*, or go straight on to *Phase 2: Later Sentences and Extras*.

Phase 1: Early Sentences. We start with the four sentence rules that children usually pick up first and provide charts that help you select sentences suitable for your child to learn. Then we describe a further six rules, with charts to identify your child's sentences, and we explain how to choose sentences that will take your child on to the next stage and widen his range of sentence constructions.

GO

Talking in sentences. Children do not take easily to talking in sentences. If they can get by with one word, why should they bother with the extra mental effort involved in thinking up sentences? Hence we shall describe how you might entice your child to start combining words. Once this hurdle is overcome, most children seem to develop their own momentum. This is sometimes described as the 'explosive' phase of acquiring language. Nonetheless, the child is still dependent on you for example and encouragement. We shall describe some very ordinary and enjoyable activities that are particularly suitable for language growth.

POSTSCRIPT

Phase 2: Later Sentences and Extras. We show you how children make longer and longer sentences by combining the two-word rules they have already learnt. It is also during this time that children start to use the small extra words adults use—'the', 'a', 'is', 'be'. On their own, they are pretty meaningless, but they serve a vital function in our daily conversation, as you will see later. Likewise, children have to learn the ways of changing the meaning of a word by adding extra sounds to it—for instance, '-ed' added to the action word 'jump' means it happened in the past, but add 's' and the action happens in the present. However, if you are talking about *a* jump in horse racing and you add an 's', then it means more than one jump—two jumps. If you are slightly confused by all this, think how children must feel. But they will not be fluent speakers of their mother tongue until they have mastered these extra rules and learnt to apply them. For example, in proper English we do not say 'the mouses runned up the clock'—even though we get the meaning. We shall outline ways of helping your child to become a more sophisticated language user.

| ON YOUR MARKS |

BASIC SENTENCE RULES

'Very sentence within of ordering, the important is words a.' Sorry, that should read 'The ordering of words within a sentence is very important.' Every time you open your mouth to speak, your mind 'whirls' through a host of 'do's' and 'don'ts'. But you are so expert at these you do it quite unconsciously. However, if you hear people break a rule, you will spot it straight away and, like as not, they will quickly correct themselves—like the football commentator who, in a fit of enthusiasm, said, 'The bar's hit the ball,' rather than 'The ball's hit the bar.' The newspaper headline that reads 'Man bites dog' will tell a different story from the more usual 'Dog bites man'.

In English the convention is that the person or thing doing the action (i.e. the actor or subject) comes before the action word or verb: ball hits . . . man bites; whereas the object (or person) having the action done to it or him, comes after the verb: hits bar . . . bites dog. If you get these rules mixed up, then not only do you change the meaning but you also cause confusion in your listeners. Could the unlikely meaning really be true?

Tennis umpire abuses John McEnroe
The kangaroo eats Prince Philip
American President becomes old lady

There is yet another rule used in the above examples—did you spot it? If you want further to describe a person or an object, the adjectives must come before its name. Hence it is *tennis* umpire, not umpire tennis, or *old* lady, not lady old. In English, we highlight what is special about the person or object by mentioning this first.

There are many other rules for combining words, some of which we shall study in more detail later, but at this point we want to recap on the advantages of talking in sentences, rather than in single words.

1 *Sentences let you communicate your intentions more clearly*
For example, if your child just says 'sweet' he could mean

'there's a sweet' or 'give me a sweet' or 'where's my sweet gone?' But if he uses a sentence—even just a two-word sentence—his meaning is immediately clear to everyone: 'there sweet', 'me sweet', 'where sweet?' This makes for far less frustration all round.

2 *We can describe situations more precisely by combining words into sentences*
Imagine what it would be like if you had to learn a new word to describe every action, depending on who was doing it—thus a man eating might be '*genate*', a woman eating '*teawom*', a dog eating '*towdef*', and so on; and then there would be a whole set of new words once the action changed—'namog' would be 'man gone'. Such a language would take ages to learn and one wonders if our memories would be up to it. We have adopted instead a much more efficient approach based around sentence rules. For instance, if you remember the rule 'name of actor + action' and the names of ten people and ten actions, then you can create 100 different sentences (ten times ten) . . . man eat, girl eat, man wash, girl wash, etc. You do not have to learn each sentence singly.

The efficiency is even greater when you want to be more precise and say what the 'actors' are eating or washing. Using a second rule, 'Action plus object of action', and knowing another ten names of objects, 1,000 different sentences can be created . . . man eat apple, girl wash pear, etc. Thus, rules let us generate precise meanings with little extra effort of memory.

3 *Sentence rules enable you to invent your own ways of conveying meanings*
Better still, combining words lets you invent totally new sentences. For example, one child, on seeing a bald man, turned to his mother and said, 'Hair gone.' It is extremely unlikely that the child had ever before heard such a sentence, so he was not imitating or remembering a past event. Rather, he created his own sentence to express a meaning for which he did not have a word. Such creative language is frequently used by children when they are lost for words and it is exploited to the full by some writers and poets who want to jolt us into thinking more deeply about what they are trying to convey: 'My love is like a red, red rose', 'Bridge over troubled water'.

One consequence is that you can end up with sentences that are meaningless except in a fantasy world.
'Hey diddle diddle, the cat and the fiddle, The cow jumped over the moon. The little dog laughed to see such fun and the dish ran away with the spoon.'
To make sense, both the words and their order have to be attuned.

4 *Sentences let you talk about the past and the future*
Possibly one of the greatest features of language is that it can be used to refer to things that have happened in the past or that will occur in the future. Other animals can only communicate about their present experiences. Children are rather like this, too, when they start to talk and, although it is possible to converse in single words about past or future experiences, it can become very confusing. It is so much easier when sentences are used and the appropriate verb and tense chosen. 'Last week we *went* on the train. Next Sunday we *shall go* to the zoo.'
In short then,

| Sentences let children make their meaning very clear. |

No longer does the listener have to guess or puzzle out the children's intentions from the context, or from what they know of them. The children themselves make perfect sense.

What is a sentence?
At its simplest, a sentence is two or more words which *the speaker has put together*. Note the last phrase. We recall a teacher who claimed that a pupil often talked in sentences. To prove it she produced a picture of a footballer and asked the boy, 'Who's this?' 'Man,' came the reply . . . 'What's he doing?' 'Kicking,' said the boy . . . 'What's he kicking?' 'Ball,' was the answer. 'That's right, man kicking the ball.' 'You see', said the teacher turning to us, 'he can talk in sentences.' But it was the teacher who put the words together for that boy. He was speaking only in single words. Beware of making the same mistake with your child.

Ready for sentences
Children do not suddenly start to talk in sentences. They

prepare for it well in advance of ever putting two words together. We shall now describe the signs that will let you know when children are ready to begin.

Understanding relationships. Sentences combine two or more ideas. They describe a relationship. At the one-word stage the child focuses on only one idea at a time, e.g. 'teddy' (if he sees a teddy) or 'fall' (if he sees it falling). However, the two-word sentence, 'teddy fall', more accurately describes what is happening. In order to produce this type of sentence, the child has to be able to *recognise* the relationship between the two elements and mentally combine the ideas of 'teddy' and 'falling'. If he can only attend to one idea at a time—as is the case with all babies and young infants—then sentences are beyond him.

Two good indications of readiness are:

* The child often creates relationships in his play. For example, washes the doll, then teddy, then himself, or sorts the big blocks from the little blocks.

  (See Section Three for further details and ideas for encouraging these play activities.)

* The child regularly follows your suggestions for combining two or more ideas out of a range of alternatives. For example, if you say, 'Put the hat on teddy', the child correctly selects a hat and the teddy bear from among his playthings. (Remember, no pointing or clues allowed.) Likewise, if you say, 'Bring me the dirty plates', when there is a choice of clean plates and dirty ones, and he gets it right nearly every time, then he is beginning to understand relationships.

Knowing words. It is obvious that children must know words before they can combine them into sentences—the minimum would be two, 'Bye' and 'mummy', but in fact children usually have a vocabulary of 30-plus words before they begin joining them into sentences. There is no definite number and, anyway, it is not the total number of words that is important but the different *types* of words a child know and uses. Thus a boy who knows 30 words, but only names of people and objects, is not as well off as the girl who knows 30 words that include action, social and modifying words.

* As a rough guideline, you could start to expect your child to talk in sentences when he regularly uses 30-plus words drawn from at least three categories on the First Words form (p. 163). If your child has not reached that point yet, you should continue with the activities listed in Section Five.

Listening to your child. There are several other indications that your child is close to talking in sentences, which you can pick up by listening to him.

* *Copies your sentences*—Your child may immediately copy what you say, even though he does not come out with his own sentences. Sometimes children abbreviate. You say 'washing your hands' and the child replies 'wash hands'. This is an excellent sign that the child is not merely parroting, but has translated your meaning into the words he already knows—admittedly with a clue or two from you.

* *Adds on a sound*—Another indicator—which is easier to pick up from a tape-recording than at the time—is the child's tendency to add a sound on to a word. Children seem to know that something extra is needed, but they cannot quite manage two proper words—one and a half

must suffice. 'Mummy beh' for 'Mummy brush', or 'me de' for 'me play'.

Changing intonation. The way we say words—the intonation we use—is another indication to the listener of our meaning. For instance, 'sw . . . eet', spoken with a rising tone at the end, becomes a question ('Are you really going to eat a sweet?'). If the tone is rather more demanding, it will mean, 'Give me a sweet', and if you are pointing to a sweet you will state it rather more matter of factly. If you can spot these sort of variations in the way your child uses *words* (they may even be present in his babble), then it is a sign he does appreciate different meanings but is constrained in expressing them by his inability to form sentences. However, this in itself becomes an incentive to learn the new skill.

False start. Finally, beware of the false start, when children appear to be combining words into sentences but are merely repeating standard phrases they have heard you use—'good boy' 'go away' or 'cup of tea'. The child is not combining the two ideas for himself, but treating them as though they were all one word. After all, there are words like ban-an-a and rad-i-o (which have three parts to them), so why not words like 'cupoftea'? It is a good sign when your child starts to use phrases of this type, so be on the lookout for sentences that he has created. It is hard sometimes to tell the difference between a standard *phrase* and a child's own sentence. These guidelines might help:

More likely a PHRASE if . . .	*More likely a SENTENCE if . . .*
* You (or the family) often say this.	* You rarely, if ever, say this.
* There is no pause between the words.	* The child pauses between the words in the sentence.
* The child rarely breaks the phrase into separate words or varies the word order (e.g. says 'cup of tea' but never 'cup of milk' or 'pot of tea').	* The child links the same words in different combinations (e.g. 'mummy teeth', 'brush teeth', 'mummy brush').

In sum, then, you will know your child is ready for sentences when:
* he shows an understanding of relationships in his play or by following your requests;
* he regularly uses 30+ words from at least three different categories on the *First Words* Form;
* he copies your sentences, adds extra words to his single words or varies the intonation of the word according to the meaning he wants to express;
* he uses standard phrases as though they were a single word.

These are the foundations for building sentences. It is worth ensuring that these skills are well established before expecting your child to talk in sentences. If the foundations are shaky, the building may never get off the ground.

Acquiring sentences

Children have a lot to learn about forming sentences. We have broken this down into two phases. Although they overlap, it does mean you can focus on the phase that is most appropriate to your child.

PHASE 1: *Early Sentences*
On p. 191 we describe the four sentence rules that children usually acquire first, or which are relatively easy to teach. If your child is not putting words together as yet, this is where you will begin. A further six sentence rules are also described in this section (on p. 197) which will, with the previous four, enable the child to construct sentences of three or more words.

PHASE 2: *Later Sentences and Extras*
In this phase, children start to combine the two-word rules they learnt in Phase 1, to produce sentences of three words and longer. Another feature of this phase is the 'extras'. By this, we mean the additional words or sounds that we use to transform children's telegram-like sentences—'daddy hammer wall'—into proper sentences—'daddy *is* hammer*ing the* wall.'

We shall describe each phase in more detail later on in the section and explain ways of helping your child to learn more about sentences. But before you read about the phases, we should like you to carry out the activity given in the following pages. The information you collect will be needed when you come to read about the two phases.

GET SET

MONITORING YOUR CHILD'S PROGRESS

Over the next few days, we should like you to fill in the special chart shown on p. 189. Write in examples of the sentences you hear your child use, under the appropriate column. Enlist the family's help—make a copy of the chart and put it up in the living room, so that they can add to it. You need only write down a sentence once. If your child repeats the same sentence, or says it over and over, you can either ignore it or, if you want to have a full record, place a tick against the sentence every time it is spoken. You should fill in the chart as follows:

One-element sentences—In this column you should write in:
   a)   Standard phrases the child uses that sound like two-word sentences but are not, e.g. all gone, come here, fall down. Remember, these count as one word if they occur in longer sentences, thus, 'com'ere mum' is a two-word sentence.
   b)   Sentences spoken by the child with only one word distinct. Try to think what the child meant the other words to be. These could be added in brackets thus, 'mummy mieh' (more?)
   c)   Sentences that the child copied you saying, but write down *exactly* what the child *said* and mark it with I, thus: (Adult said, 'Now go away, doggie'). Child said, 'Go'way doggie I.
Two-word sentences—List in this column sentences with *two* clear words that the child thought of by himself, i.e. not imitating you (spontaneous usage).
Three-word (or more) sentences—Sentences that have three or more clear words in them should be listed here. Remember, if the child uses a stereotyped phrase—'cup-of-tea, please'— this would count as a two-word sentence.
Sentences with extra words and/or sounds added—If your child starts to use the small extra words like 'the, is, am', or adds the sounds 's' or 'd' to a word to indicate plural, possessive or past tense, write these sentences in this column, e.g. 'Rabbit runn*ing*', 'more biscuit*s* please', 'throw*ed the* truck'. Remember,

CHART 1: SENTENCES

Child's name:............   Number of days covered by chart:............

ONE-ELEMENT SENTENCES	TWO-WORD SENTENCES	THREE-WORD (or more) SENTENCES	SENTENCES WITH EXTRA WORDS AND/OR SOUNDS ADDED

these should be sentences the child thinks of for himself. If he is copying you, write them in under the first column.

What the chart tells you
After two or three days, look over the chart and find which one of the sections below applies to your child.

No entries on the chart or fewer than ten items under column 1
Your child is not ready to move on to sentences. Yout time would be better spent in helping him to get ready, by continuing with the activities suggested in earlier sections. If you are convinced that your child is ready, but he just did not say as much over the past few days as he usually does, then keep on with the chart for another day or so. It is not in your child's best interests to rush on too quickly.

Ten or more items recorded but only in column 1
Although your child is not combining words by himself, it does look as though he is ready to begin, provided that,
* he has 30 or more words recorded on his *First Words* form from at least *three* different categories;
* he understands relationships (see p. 184);
* he is using words to ask for things and not merely imitating you.

If you cannot answer 'yes' to the above three points, it might be better to wait a while before starting on sentences. If the answer is 'yes', you can go on to *Phase 1: Early Sentences* (p. 191).

Items recorded in columns 1, 2 and 3.
You can confidently start to help your child learn more about combining words into sentences. We suggest you examine in more detail the sentences your child is using. You should read *Phase 1: Early Sentences* (p. 191 and *Phase 2: Later Sentences and Extras* (p. 213).

Items recorded in column 4, as well as columns 2 and 3
Your child has started to pick up the extra words and sounds used in sentences. This is something you should encourage and the section *Phase 2: Later Sentences and Extras* (p. 213), will give you some ideas. There may, however, be some rules that your child has still not mastered. Hence we recommend that

you take a closer look at the types of sentences your child used over the past few days. Please read Phase 1 (p. 191) and Phase 2 (p. 213).

PHASE 1: EARLY SENTENCES

Children's earliest sentences are made up of two words. Later they will manage three words, then four and so on. What you may not know is that, even when they are putting just two words together, they do this according to certain rules. Even the beginners do not form a sentence from any two words. The rules they learn at the two-word stage are those they will use throughout the rest of their lives.

Let us start by looking at the rules for combining words that are usually learnt early in life.

On the *First Words* form (page 163), we have five categories of words. One of the main reasons for this is that sentence rules are based around word categories. They state that you take a word from one category, add it to a word from another and you have made a particular type of sentence. Here are the four early sentence rules:

1   SOCIAL WORD + NAME OF A PERSON
2   ACTION WORD + NAME OF OBJECT/PERSON (*to which the action is done*)
3   PERSON/OBJECT NAME + ACTION WORD (*for the action they are doing*)
4   MODIFYING WORD + NAME OF PERSON/OBJECT

You might try the following activity. Look at your child's *First Words* form (p. 163) and write in the boxes overleaf six to ten sentences he *could* be saying of each type. That is, you have to use the above rules to make up possible sentences from among the words your child uses. Remember, you are thinking about *possible* sentences. He need not have spoken them.

You see, there is no shortage of sentences that can be created from even a small number of words, all of which are meaningful, if somewhat childish.

We have chosen to focus on these four rules first for the following reasons:

* They are the rules that occur early in all children's

RULE	EXAMPLE	MY CHILD COULD BE SAYING
Social Word + *Name of person*	Bye, mummy Nite, nite, teddy Yes, daddy	
Action + *Object Acted Upon*	Drink tea Wash face Kiss daddy	
Name of Person/Object + *Action*	Teddy eat Shoe off Car go	
Modifying Word + *Person/Object/ Action*	Big drink That dress More in	

development of language and the ideas conveyed by these
sentences occur in many other languages as well as English.
* They are rules that are *useful* for the child because, by using
them, he will be able to generate sentences that clearly
express his needs and wants.
* These rules are the basis for more complex sentences. For
example, by combining the rules 'Person + Action' and
'Action + Object' the child can form three-word sentences of
the type 'Person + Action + Object' (me eat sweets). Other
combinations of rules will produce longer sentences—No,
mummy, eat my sweets. (Social word + Person: Action +
Modifier + Object).
* These sentence rules are easier to teach children than some
of those we shall consider later. Hence they can be used to
get children starting to join words together.

Practice activity

The following activity will help you to understand better the rules children use in making up sentences. Chart 2 (p. 194) lists the four main rules we described earlier. 'Other sentences' are those that do not fit into any of the four rules.

Listed below are ten sentences that a father recorded for his child. We want you to decide on the rule or rules the child used for each. Write the number of the rule (1–5) beside each sentence or record it on the form, First, however, a few points to remember:

In deciding on the rule, do not be misled by the order in which the child says the words.

For example, 'bye car' and 'car bye' would count as the same sentence and be entered under rule 1, 'Social Word + Object'. Likewise, in action-word sentences, do not rely on word order to distinguish between rules 2 and 3. Rather, you have to interpret the child's meaning according to the situation, e.g. 'wash Roy' would be 'Action + Object' if the child was washing Roy but classed as 'Person + Action' if the child wanted Roy to do the action. In short, go by the child's *meaning*; not grammatical convention or adult usage.

Three-word sentences can be divided into their rules, e.g. 'want cup please' would be regarded as both 'Action + Object' (rule 2) and Social word + Object (rule 1).

CHILD SAID . . .	CONTEXT	WHICH RULE?
Nice doggy	(Pats the dog)	——
Nite-nite nana	(Going to bed)	——
Bike fall	(Hears noise outside)	——
Yes mummy	(Answers question)	——
More in	(Wants more sugar on cereal)	——
Shut door	(Brother leaves the room)	——
Daddy paper	(Brings newspaper in)	——
Mummy look	(Calling mum)	——
Wash dirty hands	(Playing at sink)	—— and ——
Wash legs daddy	(In bath)	—— and ——

Compare your answers with those given on the sample chart. If you disagree with us, try to puzzle out why this arose.

Sample of Completed Chart

CHART 2: SENTENCE RULES

Name:.................................. Date:....................................

RULE	SENTENCES CHILD USED
1 *Social Word* + *Person/Object*	mummy look nite-nite nana yes mummy
2 *Action Word* + *Object/Person*	wash (dirty) hands shut door wash legs (daddy)
3 *Person/Object* + *Action*	bike fall daddy wash (legs)
4 *Modifier* + *Object/Person*	nice doggy (wash) dirty hands
5 *Other Sentences*	daddy paper more in

CHART 2: SENTENCE RULES

Name:................................... Date:.....................................

RULE	SENTENCES CHILD USED
1 *Social Word* + *Person/Object*	
2 *Action Word* + *Object/Person*	
3 *Person/Object* + *Action*	
4 *Modifier* + *Object/Person*	
5 *Other* *Sentences*	

Activity: your child's sentences

So what rules, if any, is your child using? Look back at Chart 1 (p. 189) and the sentences you have listed under the two- and three-word columns. If there are none, you can skip this activity and go on to *'Picking new sentences'* (p. 198).

Completing Chart 2 for your child. You should do this in the same way as the practice activity above. Start with the sentences you have recorded on Chart 1 (p. 189).

1   Write in the sentence your child used in the appropriate row of the form.

2   Three-word sentences can be broken down into their different rules. However, if you can only spot one rule being used, then that is the one to record.

3   In deciding on the rule, do not be misled by the order of words. Go by the child's *meaning*, not grammatical convention.

4   If your child's sentences do not fit into any of the four rules, note it in the row called *'other sentences'*.

Compare with the example of a completed chart on page 194.

Remember to record only those sentences which your child thought of for himself. Imitations of what you said do *not* go on this form.

Needless to say, as you hear your child using other sentences, these, too, can be added to the form.

What the form tells you. You are now able to identify the rules which your child:

1   knows well (ten or more sentences noted with different words used in each);

2   the ones he is just beginning to use (just a few sentences recorded with perhaps the same word cropping up in each);

3   those he is not using at all (the row is blank)

We can now start to guide you in ways of helping your child to learn more sentences.

If, however, you have noted ten or more sentences in the 'other sentences' row of your child's chart, you should first read the next part on six more two-word rules. Indeed, this may be of interest to all readers because young children do not stick to the four rules we have described although they are the most commonly used in the early stages. However, if you want to skip this detail, you can go on to p. 198, *'Picking new sentences'*.

More two-word rules

There are six other rules that children can use to join words together, some of them adaptations of the previous four:

5 NAME OF PERSON/OBJECT (doing an action) + NAME OF PERSON/OBJECT (having action done to them), e.g. daddy paper, me dishes, mummy baby.

Here the child has missed out the action word that should come between the two names, viz. daddy *read* paper, me *wash* dishes, mummy *kiss* baby.

6 NAME OF PERSON + NAME OF OBJECT THEY POSSESS (e.g. my car, mummy dress, teddy leg).

This is a special type of modifier + object rule, in that it tells you to whom the object belongs.

In proper English, the sentence would be mummy*'s* dress or teddy*'s* leg but children very often ignore the 's' sound after the person (a point we shall come back to later). Hence, children can say the same two words but mean two different things because they have different rules in mind. For instance, 'mummy shoe' could mean 'that is mummy's shoe' (Rule 6) or 'mummy put on your shoes (Rule 5). You need to know what was going on when the child spoke, in order to determine which meaning was intended. However, this problem would not arise if the child could use longer sentences.

7 NAME OF PERSON/OBJECT + LOCATION WORD

Obvious examples are 'book there', 'here pen'. Others would be 'daddy chair' in reply to 'where's daddy?' (he's on the chair) 'dog table' (the dog's under the table). Once again, these two words could have other meanings like 'it's daddy's chair' (Rule 6).

8 ACTION WORD + LOCATION

This time the child is being more specific about the action— 'sit there', 'come here', 'go under'. Again, they may not be so clear—'sit (on the) bed' or 'jump (over the) rope'. Previously we have included these sentences under Rule 2, but it would be more correct to include them here.

Finally, there are two rules that children use to convey a specific message:

9   NEGATION + NAME OF OBJECT/EVENT
'No wee-wee', 'no want', 'go away, doggie'. The words may vary but the idea of 'not wanting' comes across very precisely with this rule.

10   QUESTION WORD + NAME OF PERSON/OBJECT/EVENT
'Where spoon?' 'What this?' 'where go?' From sentences of this type, it is quite clear that the child is seeking information. Remember, too, that at an earlier stage they could ask questions by varying the tone of voice—'My dinner?' 'Going out?' but these count as Rules 4 and 8 respectively. (See Section Two for further details on children's messages.)

The ten rules we have mentioned are not the only ones, but we think you have enough to be going on with. They are certainly the ten most used rules and with them children can create literally thousands of sentences.

Your child's sentences
Chart 3 enables you to identify the other sentences your child may be using. You should complete this in the same way as Chart 2 (see instructions on page 196).

Once you have done this, it will give you ideas about new types of sentences you could pick for your child to learn.

Do not worry if your child comes out with sentences that do not fit into any of our ten types. These soon disappear as the child gets a firmer grasp of the 'proper' rules used in the language he is learning.

Picking new sentences
No matter how many sentences you have recorded on Charts 2 and 3, there are plenty of others that your child could be using. For example, you might compare the sentences you wrote down on page 192 with those that your child has been heard to use (Charts 2 and 3).

Here, we shall give you guidelines on which *particular*

CHART 3: SENTENCE RULES

Child's name:........................ Date:...................................

RULE	SENTENCES CHILD USED
5 *Person/Object +* *(Action Missing)* *Person/Object*	
6 *Name of Person* *+* *Object They* *Possess*	
7 *Person/Object* *+* *Location Word*	
8 *Action* *+* *Location*	
9 *Negation* *+* *Person/Object/* *Action*	
10 *Question Word* *+* *Person/Object/* *Action*	

sentences to concentrate on with your child. As we have stressed in previous sections, it is much easier for you to see progress if you work on two or three specific targets at a time. Your starting point, as always, is your child's present level of performance.

Steps in selecting sentences

1   Concentrate on one type of sentence at a time.

2   Start with a rule that your child is presently using and extend it to other words. You can do this in two ways:

    a)   If the child has said 'nite-nite, nana', you could concentrate on other 'nite-nite' sentences, i.e. 'nite-nite . . . mummy . . . daddy . . . Paul', and so forth.

    b)   You could link the names of people with other social words: 'Look, mummy . . . nana . . . Paul'.

3   If your child is *not* using any two-word sentences, we suggest you pick a social sentence, as they are among the easiest to learn and very often the child is already using gestures to indicate his meaning, e.g. points and says 'mummy' could become 'look, mummy'.

4   Ensure that the words needed for these sentences are ones your child knows and uses, i.e. they should be ticked on the *First Words* form under the Spontaneous column (p. 163).

5   Ensure that the child understands the relationship expressed in the sentences, i.e. he is an active participant in the situation, such as waving nite-nite to different people, or shows understanding in his play with toys.

6   Pick sentences that are meaningful and useful for the child's everyday life and, ideally, also reflect his interests. One test is to ask yourself, how often is my child likely to use this sentence? If you reply, hardly ever, then better think of another.

7   If your child has a range of sentences listed for one rule, then it is best to pick another sentence rule. We suggest you do this according to the numbers we gave to the rules, i.e. children generally acquire Rules 1 and 2 before 3; 3 before 4 and so on.

When you have made your selection, you might complete a chart like the sample shown opposite. This will remind you and your family of the sentences you can model for your child

SAMPLE OF NEW SENTENCES CHART

Child's name: ......Laura................... Date:......19th June......

Rules I am concentrating on write in at top of column)	RULE SOCIAL WORD + PERSON/OBJECT	RULE ACTION + OBJECT	RULE SOCIAL WORD + OBJECT	RULE ACTION + OBJECT
In each column, list 5 or 6 possible sentences for each rule	Nite-nite mummy Nite-nite Paul Nite-nite teddy Nite-nite Rupert	Wash hands Wash legs Wash face Wash cup Wash dish Wash spoon	Give me cup Give me dish Give me spoon Give me drink Give me sugar Give me pop	Kiss daddy Kiss teddy Kiss nana Kiss hands Kiss lips Kiss face

NEW SENTENCES CHART

Child's name: .... Date: ....

Rules I am concentrating on write in at top of column)	RULE	RULE	RULE	RULE
In each column, list 5 or 6 possible sentences for each rule				

and the ones you could listen out for. Please do not feel you have to fill all four columns. They are there if you want to use them.

Try to include the same words in two or more columns. This will further ensure your child gets the idea of combining words. Thus, in our example we have 'wash *cup*, give me *cup*, nite-nite, *daddy*, kiss *daddy*'.

GO

TALKING IN SENTENCES

You will be pleased to learn that most of the hard work has been done by the time you arrive at this point. In our experience, once you have decided on the *right* sentences for your child, it is a relatively simple matter of helping him to acquire the rule—at least in terms of what you can do. This is no guarantee that your child will find it easy to grasp the rule, but that may be because the rule or the particular sentences you have chosen are not the right ones for that time (see later). The approach we recommend you to use is much the same as the one you have been using to get across the meaning of words (see Section Five). Hence you will not have to learn many new skills—rather you will be updating existing ones.

We identified three stages in helping children acquire the meaning of words. Now we have added a fourth.

STEP 1: GRASPING THE MEANING (NB the child need not talk)
STEP 2: CHILD CHOOSES TO IMITATE YOU
STEP 3: CHILD THINKS OF ONE WORD WITHOUT HELP
STEP 4: CHILD THINKS OF A TWO-WORD SENTENCE BY HIMSELF

We shall describe how you can work through these four steps with your child, paying particular attention to the first. Although we shall give you lots of examples of how you might encourage children to talk in sentences, you will also have to think of your own ways of getting across the new sentences that you have picked for your child.

Step 1: Grasping the meaning

The first step, as always, is the most important. How can you help your child appreciate the meaning of sentences? There are two ways:

1 Let your child perform the sentences in his actions. For example, as he loads the washing machine, he experiences handling different sorts of clothing, along with the action of putting them into the machine. Likewise, he can pretend to feed a doll with bread, biscuits and chocolate. In each instance, he is creating, through his actions, the sentence rule you want

him to learn. Children need to be well practised at doing this before we can expect them to say the word. If possible, then, choose activities which naturally have lots of repeated actions in them with different people or objects, so that the chld can 'experience' the meaning of the sentences.

2 As the child performs the actions, you can say the appropriate sentence: 'sock in' . . . 'pants in' . . . 'shirt in' or 'eat bread' . . . 'eat biscuit' . . . etc. Try to keep your models *simple*, reducing them even to just two words. This means speaking in the way your child begins to use sentences, so that it is easier for him to copy your example.

You need not talk like this all the time, but we believe it is best to do so when you want your child to pick up new words and sentences.

Choose an activity for your child
The sentences you have picked (see p. 201) could occur by chance in everyday activities, but rather than waiting for them, we think it is better to select two or three situations where you can ensure that they will arise. This will give your child the opportunity of repeated practice and the chance to realise that these sentences apply in different settings.

It may seem rather difficult to think of enough different activities for the sentences children could create. And, indeed, it would be if you needed a new activity for every sentence. The secret is to start with your child's favourite activities and see whether you can use them to illustrate the sentence you have chosen. Below, in Chart 4, are some examples of what we mean. In each case we have chosen the less obvious sentence—there are other possibilities you may think of for yourself.

CHART 4: TWO-WORD SENTENCES

FAVOURITE ACTIVITY	POSSIBLE SENTENCES	VARIATION OF ACTIVITY
Playing with model cars trucks, etc.	1 *Wash* + name	Pretend to wash cars, trucks, bus, motorbike. Sample sentences 'wash car', 'wash bus', etc.

FAVOURITE ACTIVITY	POSSIBLE SENTENCES	VARIATION OF ACTIVITY
	2 Name + *down*	Let cars, trucks, etc., roll down an incline, e.g. a tray against a chair. Sample sentences 'car down', 'truck down', 'bus down', 'lorry down'.
	3 *my* + name	Use two shoe boxes as 'houses' with your set of models and the child. You can talk of 'my car', 'my house', 'my bus', etc.
Bath-time	1 *Gimme* + name	Child has to reach out for the objects he wants to with; 'gimme duck', 'gimme ball', etc.
	2 *Where* + name	Take it in turns to play a game of hiding objects in the water—preferably under soap-suds or foam. Sample sentences 'where's duck?' 'where's bottle?'
	3 Person + *drink*	Pretending to give drinks to dolls, plastic toys animals, etc., as well as mum and dad. Sample sentences 'duck drink', 'mummy drink.' (This is all the more fun if mum or dad dislikes it and pretends to scold the child. He is likely to give you a second and third helping!
Shopping	1 Bye-bye + name	As you pass people or objects, say 'bye-bye' to them. (Encourage the child to wave to each one—'bye-bye, bus' 'bye-bye, doggy'.)

FAVOURITE ACTIVITY	POSSIBLE SENTENCES	VARIATION OF ACTIVITY
	2 Name + in	Let your child put your purchases into the trolley as you say 'milk in', 'bread in', etc. You can do this, too, when filling up a bag with fruit— 'apple in', etc.
	3 This/that + name	Hold up two objects for child to choose—'Which one?' 'This apple' . . . 'this sweet'.
Setting the table	1 Possessive + objects	If each member of the family has his or her own place at the table, you can talk about 'mummy's' cup', 'daddy's cup', 'Mary's knife', etc., as the child sets the table.
	2 Dirty + name of object	Mix some dirty cutlery in with the clean ones. Point out the dirty ones and encourage the child to put them into the sink to be washed. As he does, you repeat 'dirty spoon', dirty fork', etc.
	3 More + name	Hand over the objects to the child one at a time, saying, 'more spoon', 'more knife', 'more fork', etc.

Same sentence—different situation
As with learning words, it is important for children to hear the same sentence being used in different situations. Here are some examples of how you might do this for some of the early sentences.

HELLO + name of person:
1 Welcoming people to the house or the children as they come to playgroup.
2 Looking at photo-album or book and saying 'Hello' to each person when they appear.
3 Pretend play with lots of characters—dolls, soft toys. Have a pretend 'door'—cut out of shoe box—for the dolls to knock on and enter through.

Object/Person + GONE:
Dinner time—As child clears the table, make a point of the empty cups, glasses and plates, saying, 'dinner gone', 'milk gone', 'tea gone'.
Hiding games—Have three containers on the floor and take it in turns to hide an object in one, saying 'teddy gone'. It is then up to the other person to find it. Repeat with other objects so that various sentences are modelled. This game can also be played at the beach—finding bucket or spade, or even daddy's feet in the sand.
Car journeys—Point out things to the child; as they disappear, say 'bike gone', 'policeman gone' and so on.

Object + *OFF:*
Undressing—As the child takes off each garment, you can model the appropriate sentence—'shoe off', 'sock off', 'pants off'. It is fun, too, if the child can undress you! You can wear a hat, scarf, slippers, gloves.
Containers—Let the child play with some tight-fitting lids on saucepans, containers with screw tops or felt-pens with caps. This gives you scope for sentences like 'lid off', 'top off', 'cap off'. If the child cannot manage to remove the lid on his own, you could expect him to say 'lid off' before you do it for him.
Clothes horse or line—Give the child the job of transferring the clothes from the line to the ironing basket. You can supply the sentences as appropriate—'hankie off', 'pants off', etc.

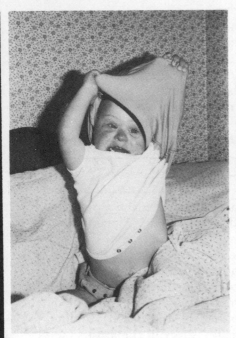 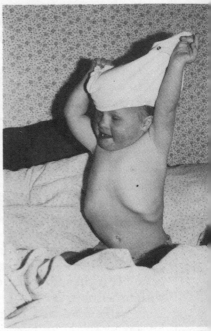

NO + Object/person/action:
Choice of foods—At snack times, offer the child a choice of
something you know he does not like and something he
does. When he refuses, say 'no jelly'. Repeat a couple of
times before offering the preferred foodstuff.
People—If the child is involved in an enjoyable activity,
threaten to take him away, e.g. on swing, in bath,
watching television. The child's response is 'no, daddy
. . . no, mummy . . .' This gives the child practice in
expressing what he *does not* want to happen.
Actions—This time the child uses the sentence to stop
something he does not like. For example, being splashed
at the swimming or paddling pool—'no splash' . . . 'no
kicking . . .' If mum tells dad, 'no splashing', it serves as a
model for the child.

SORE + name of body part:
Rough and tumble play—As you roll around, pretend to be hurt and say 'sore head', 'sore hand', etc. Child might pretend to 'hit' you and then it is your turn to hit him.
Doll play—Put plasters as bandages on parts of the doll and use words as appropriate—'sore leg' . . . 'sore arm . . .'
Outdoor play—If your child falls when playing in the garden, etc., make a point of saying 'sore knee' . . . sore hand . . .', etc.

Picking activities for your child
We hope these examples will have given you ideas for activities you can use with your child. Look back at the new sentences you have picked and now try to think of activities during which these sentences will occur naturally, so giving your child lots of practice in grasping the meaning of the new sentences. Try to think of three activities for each type of sentence you have chosen.

SENTENCE TYPE	SITUATIONS		
a) *Rule*	1)	2)	3)
b) *Rule*	1)	2)	3)
c) *Rule*	1)	2)	3)
d) *Rule*	1)	2)	3)

Do not forget
* During this step, *the child does not need to talk*. As long as he is actively involved, he is developing his understanding of relationships and hence sentences.
* Do not let the activity go on for too long. Stop before your child loses interest.
* Keep your sentence models short and make sure you say the sentence as the child does the appropriate action.

* Join in the activity with your child—taking turns at it, if possible.

Step 2: Child chooses to imitate you
Once the activities are under way, the time will come when the child starts to imitate your models. You can help to make it come sooner if you remember two points:
1 Give your child time to come out with the words during the activity. Leave a pause after you say the sentence and wait expectantly.
2 The child's attempt at saying the sentence may not be very good, but give lots of praise for an attempt and repeat the sentence with a smile: 'Yes, *dirty* spoon—well done!' *Do not force your child to imitate.* It will come if you give lots of examples. Make sure this step is well established before you move on to the next.

Step 3: Child thinks of one word without help
In this step, you can expect the child to think of one word by himself, while you supply the other.
* For instance, in the 'bye bye' game, you say, 'Bye bye . . .' then pause for the child to complete the sentence. To begin with this is best done after the child has copied your sentence—thus:
  > Adult: 'Bye bye, David'
  > Child: 'Bye, David'
  > Adult: 'Good boy—bye, David'
  > Adult: 'Bye bye . . .'
  > Child: 'David'.
* Or you can pause before the action in anticipation of the child saying a word. For example, before handing over an object to go in the washing machine, you look at it. The child says 'sock' and you immediately say 'sock in. Well done,' and let the child do the action.

You get the idea? You leave the children time to think of a word for themselves, but if they do not manage it within five seconds or so, you supply it and let the action continue.

Step 4: Child thinks of a two-word sentence by himself
Sometimes this will happen very quickly; at other times it may

come very slowly. In either case, it is up to your child. Do not be surprised if he never comes out with the sentence you have been modelling but instead starts using other sentences. That has happened to us quite frequently and it is something we cannot easily explain, except to say, once again, that it is up to the child! At this stage, adults should beware:

* of talking too much. By all means remain involved in the activity but gradually say less, so that your child has the chance to say more. In short, respond to what your child *says* rather than to what he does.

* of missing the child's attempt at a sentence. The chances are that your child's early sentences will be much more indistinct than when he speaks in single words. He has so many things to think about when creating a sentence, that it is not surprising that something gives, so listen carefully.

Alternatively, some children leave long pauses—'think time'—between the two words. 'Give me . . . . sweets.' You will only interrupt if you rush in too quickly or try to coax them into thinking of the word that follows.

There will be times when you may need to give the child some extra encouragement to talk in sentences. Remember, however, that the following suggestions are *for use in Step 4 only.*

1 *An interesting and intriguing game continues*—Invent a game that embodies your sentence, but only let the child play it when he says the sentence. For instance, when putting objects down a cardboard tube (e.g. a tin-foil tube), hold your hand over the opening until the child says 'car in', 'ball in', and so forth.

2 *The child gets something he wants*—You might be able to encourage your child to use a sentence when he wants something. 'Gimme drink', 'biscuit please', 'more spoons'.

3 *The child tells others what to do*—This is an excellent way of helping children realise how useful language is. In these games, you and the child take it in turns to tell each other what to do. 'Daddy kick'—'big cup'—'wash face'. At first, there may have to be two adults present—one to give the child models, the other to do what he is told. This could be mother and father or an older brother or sister.

Moving on to new sentences

* As your child starts to talk more often in sentences, you should bring your sentence charts up-to-date (p. 195 and p. 199).

* You could then pick more new sentences, following the same guidelines we outlined earlier (p. 200).

* Once again, you may think of activities to illustrate the meaning of the new sentences, or you could adapt familiar ones (p. 204).

* If your child has mastered these early sentence rules, you can move on to *Phase 2: Later Sentences and Extras.*

POSTSCRIPT
Phase 2: Later Sentences and Extras

ON YOUR MARKS

If your child is regularly using a variety of two-word sentences and occasionally produces longer sentences, then you should find this postscript helpful. Here we deal with the way children learn to produce longer sentences of three, four and more words and describe how they start to use extra words and sounds to make their meaning even clearer. We shall give you guidelines for identifying new types of sentences that your child has yet to master, along with advice on activities that will be particularly beneficial during this phase, and we suggest how you can best help your child.

If you have not already done so, you might find it useful to read through Phase 1 (p. 191). This will give you an idea of the approach we recommended for the early stages and many of the points made there apply here as well.

Longer sentences

The two-word sentence rules we described in Phase 1 are the building blocks for all the child's later sentences. Invariably these result from combinations of two-word rules. For instance, here are three examples of how children can express the same idea even more precisely by combining more rules to produce longer and longer sentences:

a) REQUESTS (Child's idea—to get the ball from daddy)	SENTENCE RULES
1 ball	—
2 daddy ball	5
3 daddy throw ball	3+2
4 daddy throw ball me	3+2+8
5 please, daddy, throw ball to me	1+3+2+to+8
6 please, daddy, throw the ball to me	1+3+the+2+to+8

b) INFORMATION (Idea—to tell   SENTENCE RULES
   mummy about my car)
   1 my   —
   2 my car   6
   3 Paul my car   5+6
   4 Paul playing my car   3+2+ing+6
   5 Paul playing my big car   3+2+6+4
   6 Paul is playing with my   3+is+2+ing+with+6+4
      big car

c) QUESTION (Idea—to get a   SENTENCE RULES
   particular comic book)
   1 comic?   —
   2 where comic?   10
   3 where Paul comic?   10+6
   4 where Paul comic no want? 10+6+9
   5 where old comic Paul   10+4+3+9
      no want?
   6 where's the old comic Paul 10+'s+the+4+3+
      doesn't want   does+9

Notice how the child's meaning becomes clearer with each new rule. By the time the children reach the stage of four- or five-word sentences, you do not have to be with them to understand what they mean. Prior to this stage, you would have had to guess at their meaning from what was going on at the time the child said the sentence. Not surprisingly, the best people at guessing correctly are the child's parents.

But did you spot another development which took place around stages 5 and 6? The child begins to make additions to the words or to put in additional words—like 'the' and 'does'. This development makes his meaning crystal-clear, mainly because it gives the listener extra clues.

Additional words and additions to words
The list given below is the approximate order in which children start to use extra sounds and words in sentences. By and large, these are used to help make the meaning clearer or to change it in a small but significant way. Children only start using these

extras when they can combine words fluently into two- or three-element sentences.

1   *Add '-ing' to action words*, e.g. runn*ing*, eat*ing*, go*ing*.
2   *Add 's' sound to names of objects or people to indicate more than one*, e.g. cup*s*, dog*s*, apple*s*.
3   *Add 's' sound to a person's name to indicate he or she owns the object*, e.g. teddy*'s* ear, Rory*'s* turn, it*'s* mummy*'s*.
4   *Use the words 'a' or 'the' before the names of objects*, e.g. hit *the* drum (. . . rather than *the* doll), give me *a* sweet (when there's more than one sweet).
5   *Add the sound 'd' to action words to indicate past tense*, e.g. he kick*ed* me, I wash*ed* my leg.
6   *Add the sound 's' to action words to indicate present tense (but only when describing people or objects other than yourself*, e.g. she kiss*es* me but I kiss her.
7   *Add words like 'am', 'is', and 'are' before action words as appropriate*, e.g. I *am* running, he *is* running, you *are* running. Sometimes these are abbreviated to I'm, he's and you're.

However, there are some notable exceptions to these rules which children also have to learn. For instance:
Irregular plurals—such as *mice* (instead of mouses), teeth (not tooths), *men* (not mans) and *sheep* (not sheeps). Children learn them as extra words and may sometimes get confused between the two possibilities, saying, 'One teeth sore'.
Irregular verbs referring to past actions—many of the words we use to describe common actions change their form when we are referring to a past happening. They do not obey the usual rule of adding 'd' to the word. Thus we say ran (run) came (come), ate (eat), went (go), sat (sit), slept (sleep), threw (throw), did (do). Children learn these as though they are new words, but do not be in a hurry to introduce them until the present form (i.e. the words in brackets above) is well understood. Incidentally, if your child mistakenly adds 'd' to any of the words, take heart—it is an excellent sign: I *goed*, he *comed* here, teddy *sitted* down. It shows they have grasped the idea of a rule that usually works.

GET SET

LISTENING TO YOUR CHILD

Over the next day or two, you should listen out for three-word sentences in particular and for any extras that your child might be using. These can be recorded in Charts 5 and 6 (pp. 217 and 218).

Another possibility is to tape-record a conversation you have with your child and go through the recording very carefully to pick up sentences and the inclusion of extras. Often we miss them in the hurly-burly of play. This information will give you a clearer idea of the new type of sentences you might start to encourage your child to use, i.e. the last column on the charts. Here are guidelines to help your selection, first for sentence types and then for the 'extras'.

Picking three-word sentences

As before we find it best to:

* concentrate on one kind of rule at a time—preferably widening a rule your child has already begun to use.

* start with the three-word sentences that combine two rules which the child already uses in two-word sentences (see Charts 2 and 3).

* choose sentences that are useful for the child to have. How often is he likely to use these sentences? If the answer is hardly ever, it may not be worth focusing on them.

You can also record or chart the new sentences you intend to concentrate on with your child. These can grow out of the activities you used during Phase 1 (see p. 203).

We have only listed some of the three-word sentences which children create; there are many other possible combinations (record them under the 'Other Sentences' on the chart) and the list would be even greater for four-word-plus sentences. However, children seem to discover these for themselves, provided they have got the basic knack of combining words into sentences—a knack that comes from your example and encouragement and with time.

CHART 5: THREE WORD SENTENCES

TYPE	EXAMPLES	SENTENCES MY CHILD HAS USED	NEW SENTENCES
Actor + Action + Object	me kick ball mummy do it daddy wash hands we play game		
Action + Modifier/ Possessive + Object/Person	wash daddy car want big sweet kick that ball smack bold daddy		
Modifier/ Possessive + Object/Person + Action	big spoon in mummy shoe gone new dress on bad dog bite		
Person/Object + Action + Location	daddy come here book fall there teddy in box mummy sit chair		
Questions (can take various forms)	where daddy go? what baby eat? who sit there? why no peas?		
Other Sentences Child Uses			

CHART 6: EXTRAS

ITEM	EXAMPLES	ALREADY USES	NEW CONTEXTS
Add 'ing' to action word	running eating going		
Add 's' to indicate more then one	caps dogs apples		
add 's' to indicate possession	mummy's Rory's teddy's		
'a' + 'the' (articles)	*the* drum *a* sweet *the* end		
Add 'd' for past action	jumped kicked washed		
Add 's' for present action	jumps washes kicks		
Add 'am', 'is' + 'are' before action	I *am* falling he *is* running you *are* coming		
Irregular plurals	mice teeth men		
Irregular past verbs, NB child uses both tenses	went (+go) sat (+sit) threw (throw)		

Picking extras

If your child has not started to use any of the extra features in his sentences, we suggest that you start from the top of Chart 6 and work down. Introduce one new feature at a time and do it within two-word sentences initially—especially those that your child knows well. Once he has grasped the idea, you can expect to hear the extra features being used in his three- or four-word sentences (assuming he has reached that stage).

If your child has already begun to use an 'extra' feature in his sentences, you should first concentrate on encouraging him to do this more often before introducing a new one. There is space on Chart 6 for you to record particular times or settings when you might try to give your child extra practice at using these features.

GO

ACQUIRING NEW SENTENCES

The ways in which you help children develop longer and more correct sentences are no different from those we discussed in Phase 1:

* Try to find two or three activities that the child enjoys and that will make clear the meaning of the new sentences.
* Give your child clear models of the sentences, placing particular emphasis on the words he is inclined to leave out, viz. '*daddy* eat peas', or 'give me *my* cup', or the extra features you want him to learn, e.g. 'kick*ing* the ball'.
* Do not expect your child to say the words on his own until he willingly copies your models.
* Respond to what your child says, even if it is an incomplete sentence and, whatever you do, do not say he is wrong if he leaves out a word or an extra feature.
* Instead, model the full sentence for him—'mummy sit *chair*'—or ask a question that identifies the missing word—'where will mummy sit?' 'Chair'. Then say the whole sentence again.
* Likewise, if the child misses out a feature, model the sentence again, repeating the feature—'runn*ing*—runn*ing* for the bus'.

Although all these suggestions will help, the most important one of all is that you expect your child to talk in fuller sentences and should show particular pleasure when he does. You will know you are starting to go places when you can have a 'conversation' with your child. Indeed, this is a sign of real progress. Listed below are some ideas of when conversations are most likely to occur. But then, no two children are alike. If some of these do not work with your child, try to think of others that might.

Looking at story books. Encourage your child to tell you part of a familiar story—you can begin quite simply by having him name the picture of the characters and build up until he tells you about the events shown in the picture—'sat on chair, chair broke, Goldilocks fall down'.

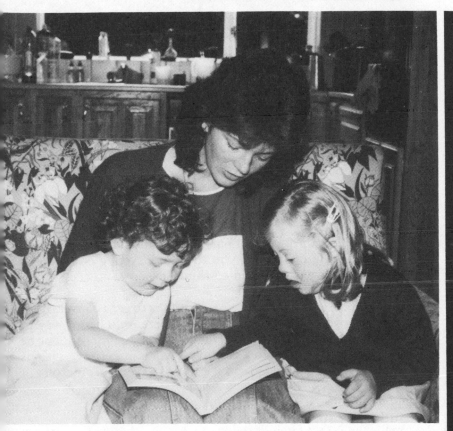

Photograph albums. These are a useful way of reliving a past event—a trip to the seaside, or a birthday party. Encourage your child to act out some of the things you did—you can give a clue or two by doing some of the actions yourself. If your child enjoys this, do not be afraid to repeat it. Children do not seem to get bored as quickly as adults and the practice helps them master more sentences.

Making something together. Another good conversational setting is when you are both working to make something. It could be baking, tidying up the room or a fun activity like making a house from lego bricks or painting. You can both talk about what you *are* doing and what you plan to do, as well as the things you like and do not like.

Table-top games. Simple games, like Snap, picture dominoes or ones with a dice are another good setting for getting conversations going. The more familiar your child is with the game the better. Make sure he really understands the rules before you expect conversations to begin.

Outings. The unfamiliar event is another source of chat. Visits to the zoo, bus trips, seaside excursions and picnics will give you and your child the chance to talk about new things. Let your child take the lead at drawing your attention to the new things. You can then supply the words to describe the event.

Make-believe play. Games in which you and the child take the part of other people can widen your conversations. You could be the shop-keeper and customer, a bus conductor and passenger, a doctor and patient, teacher and pupil. Indeed, the child can be mummy and you the child. Acting out pretend scenes can 'force' the child to think of new sentences.

The emphasis in all the above activities is to get a conversation going between you and your child. There is no better way to bring on your child's use of language and, the more adept he becomes at this, the more readily he will join in conversations with you. It is an upward spiral leading to ever more mastery of language.

Indistinct speech
When your child first starts to talk in sentences, his speech will probably become more indistinct. This is natural. He has so many things to think of—the meaning he wants to convey, the right words to use, the order they go in—that it is not surprising that something gives—clarity of speech. Moreover, he is not skilled at making the rapid movements of lips and tongue, etc., that are needed when saying one word after another.

But as your child becomes more adept at talking in sentences, you should expect his speech to become even clearer than when he was at the single-word stage. One reason is that he is forced to pay attention to the slight differences between words of very different meanings. 'Please play planes' is an example of a sentence that will improve any child's speech.

Likewise, adding an extra sound like 's' or 'ed' to a word requires clearer diction from the child if he is to be understood.

Generally, clearer speech follows once the child is able to form words fluently into sentences. We do *not* advise you to focus on how a child says a sentence until he is using words fluently in correct sequence. That is when you can begin to expect him to say the words more clearly.

Here are some pointers as to what you might do:

* *Let the child know you understand what he means but that you want him to practise saying it more clearly.*

* *Give him a clear example of how the sentence should be spoken.* Do NOT tell him 'you're wrong' or even, 'you're nearly right' and then make him say it again. He will have no clue as to what to do differently.

Do NOT copy the way your child speaks—he may think that is the correct way to talk.

Do NOT break words up into their separate sounds and have the child copy each one, e.g. ba-nan-a. This will not help him to say the whole word any more clearly.

* *Give your child time to think.* It is normal for children to leave pauses between the words or to fill the gap by repeating the word or by saying 'a-a-a-a-a'. Do not panic—he is not developing a stammer.

Remember, too, that some sounds are easier for children to make than others (see p. 149) and that children may be able to say a sound when it occurs in certain words (e.g. at the end) but not in others when it is at the beginning. This, too, will come with practice.

Your child's speech may also become more indistinct if a major change occurs in his lifestyle, such as going to pre-school. It will soon improve.

If you suspect that your child has particular problems in speaking clearly, possibly through hearing loss or for any other reason, then consult a speech therapist.

Recording progress

From time to time (say every three months) it is worth tape-recording your child's conversations and then writing out all that he says. This will let you detect the new type of sentences he is saying, the extra words and sounds he has begun to use and any improvements in the clarity of his speech. You might also like to update Charts 5 and 6 and possibly spot any other gaps that remain in his use of language.

There are still other features of language that your child has to master (see Table below) but the topsoil has been laid, the roots have taken and continued growth should occur naturally from this point.

LATER DEVELOPMENTS IN LANGUAGE GROWTH

Contractions	—'s, —'m, or —'re	they're running; he's hungry; I'm going home.
Contracted negatives	—n't	I can't do it; it isn't fair.
Order of words in questions	*is* or *are* come before person/object	where are my shoes? *not* where my shoes are? or is the water cold? *not* water is it cold?
Future tense of verbs	will, shall contraction —'ll	I will do it. Tonight we will play ball. Tomorrow you'll see granny.
Passive tense	was, were	He was hit by the ball. United were beaten by City.
Other tenses	might, may, would could	He could fall off. I might go there, too.

SECTION SEVEN: LISTEN WHO'S TALKING

This section looks at ways of extending and encouraging children's *use* of language once they have reached the stage where they can put two words together and are beginning to use longer sentences to express a wider range of messages in a variety of contexts. The adult's role in the child's world remains a very important one and there are many ways in which they can help children to extend their use of language and become more competent 'communicators'.

What you will read about in this section

ON YOUR MARKS

Extending language usage beyond the home setting. We describe how you can gradually extend your child's involvement in activities outside the home and how important these are in rounding-off his mastery of the basic skills involved in speech, language and communication.

Adults' use of language—how you can help your child. The golden rule of conversation is to be responsive to your child; follow his lead. In the case of passive children, we describe ways of encouraging them to take the initiative. We list some Do's and Don't's for adults to follow when conversing with young children.

GET SET

Listen to yourself talking. We describe an activity all adults should experience, namely listening to a tape-recording of themselves talking to a child. It is an invaluable learning exercise and the form we provide will help guide you through it.

GO

Contexts for extending children's language in conversation. We pinpoint a number of situations which are particularly fruitful in encouraging children to communicate through language. These can be used with groups of children, as well as with individuals. However, the secret of success is simply stated. Children need lots of topics to talk about and lots of opportunities for talking with an attentive listener.

ON YOUR MARKS

EXTENDING LANGUAGE USAGE BEYOND THE HOME SETTING

The child's earliest communications are inevitably exchanged with his closest care-giver but later extend, as he grows, to his immediate family—adults and siblings—and to close friends such as baby-sitters.

Gradually he moves from total reliance on gesture and random vocalisation to the stage where he can express his feelings and wants by using a limited number of single words which he slowly learns to put together to form his first sentences. His words are frequently unclear. Those who know him well are able to understand what he is trying to say only because they are tuned in to his needs and his daily routine and are familiar with his gestures and sound patterns. Often his mother can understand better what he wants than other members of his household, let alone grand-parents and neighbours who see him less frequently.

Once the child has started using sentences, the next important goal is to extend his use of language beyond his immediate, safe home setting. He has now acquired the early skills of saying words and attaching them correctly to the objects or ideas to which they refer. That is quite an achievement and, as we have explained, is easier done in a familiar, friendly environment. But children need to apply these skills when it comes to communicating a wider range of messages, and they have to learn to do this in all sorts of situations, particularly in communicating with people who are not as closely tuned in to their 'system' as are their immediate family.

This process of extending language usage is a gradual one and may vary greatly from child to child. Like us, you have probably come across children who are chatter-boxes at home but say little or nothing at playgroups or who refuse to speak to neighbours and visitors to the home. We may not fully understand why this occurs but equally we do not want it to persist for so long that it becomes a habit.

A good beginning is to make outings a regular part of your

child's life from a very young age—excursions to the shops, park or beach, to visit friends and relations and perhaps the doctor or infant welfare nurse, or to go with you to sports events, informal meetings and church, where he will see and meet other people. You and your child could get involved with parent and toddler groups—an excellent introduction to playing with other children. Later he may go to a playgroup or pre-school. Now he will spend periods of time without his parents present, interacting with other adults *and children* and having to cope with the frustrations of not always having his attempts to communicate understood. This frustration, so long as it is not so severe that it causes distress, can provide an important impetus for growth in the child's communicative skills. He wants to be understood by the people he is attempting to interact with, and will persevere in trying to make his message clear. This is a difficult stage, because in new settings there will be novel and different things to talk about. Your child will need as much help as he can get from the caring adults, and perhaps older children, with whom he is interacting.

The way in which adults can help, both when the child is acquiring the very early skills, and at this later stage when the main task is extending the range of his use of language in big-wide-world settings outside the home, will be the focus of attention in this section.

ADULTS' USE OF LANGUAGE—HOW YOU CAN HELP YOUR CHILD

A lot of people, such as linguists, psychologists and special educators, who have observed parents, but mostly mothers, interacting with their infants, believe there are a number of things most of them do that make the child's language-learning task easier; some of these things are more important than others. They have also discovered that some things adults do may make it harder for the child. We shall look first at the most important aspect—adult responsiveness—and then list a number of Do's and Don'ts.

a)   The golden rule for adults: be responsive!

'Responsiveness' is the most important quality for any adult to have when interacting with a young language-learning child. In Section Two we noted how, in infancy, the mother 'interprets' the baby's earliest sounds and movements, ascribes meaning to them, and then responds to the 'meaning' as if the child had been sending a deliberate message. In this way the infant is helped to learn how to send messages, and learns also that interacting with a caring and responsive care-giver is a satisfying experience. As the child matures, his messages become more specific and much more varied. Earliest messages generally relate to feelings of comfort and well-being, or the reverse—hunger, cold, wet and discomfort.

Once the child is mobile he will attempt to communicate about all the different things he can see and touch, about all the activities he becomes involved in, including the regular routines of his day such as meal-times, bath-time, bed-time. The range of his activities and interests makes the task of the care-giver both more demanding and more complicated. His messages will often be far from clear, and mothers are busy with a myriad activities in addition to caring for a language-learning toddler. But it is at this crucial stage that an attentive and responsive care-giver can play a tremendously important role in facilitating the child's growing capacity to communicate in different ways about an ever-increasing range of topics. A parent's responsiveness to his attempts will help ensure that he sticks to his task until he has succeeded, rather than losing heart through lack of success or through finding the effort of trying to send a message too great and unrewarding, and hence giving up altogether. A child improves his use of gestures, and acquires the sounds and words he needs, as he hears them modelled by his mother in her responsive interactions with him.

Of course, all this applies equally to playgroup leaders and teachers, to say nothing of grandparents and friends.

Here are some guidelines for 'responsiveness':

1 *Watch your child closely* in his activities and play and be ready to respond to any attempts that he makes to communicate with you, whether you are out for a walk together, feeding the dog, mixing dough for cookies, or putting teddy to bed at bedtime. When he points at a bird flying across the park you can respond by saying, 'Yes, that's a bird', or 'see the bird', or just 'bird'! As he pats teddy after putting him to bed you can say 'night-night teddy', or 'teddy sleep'. If your child is at the stage of using gestures only, he will enjoy having you participate in his activities, and if he is attempting to use sounds and words, then hearing you say clearly what he is attempting to say will assist him to clarify his own attempts.

2 *Follow the child's lead*—Because there are so many things that very young children *cannot* do, some adults try to organise and direct them in every situation. The effect of this is further to reduce the hesitant exploratory behaviour that children display, and to inhibit early attempts at interaction with both objects and important people in their environment. Thus a second, very important aspect of 'responsiveness' is to allow the child freedom to explore and to interact with those about him as best he can, and for adults to *respond* to these early attempts quickly and sensitively. Allow the child to 'lead the dance' and follow in his steps.

Too often, adults have a fixed view of what a child should attend to, or of what they think he will find interesting. They tend not to notice his focus of attention, or they brush it aside in favour of trying to get the child to focus on what interests them. The child may be fascinated by the progress of an ant in the grass, and he may not want to go on a swing or see-saw just at that moment, even if that was what they came to the park to do. He may point to the ant and look questioningly at his care-giver—perhaps wanting to know what it is called and what it is doing. Once his curiosity has been satisfied, he will happily move on to the swings or climbing frame, but if his mother insists that they keep moving, a confrontation may develop that reduces the possibility of *any* conversation taking place and may ruin the outing altogether as a pleasant, shared experience, in which plenty of opportunity for communication can take place.

Of course, this does not mean that a child can always do *what* he wishes, *when* he wishes. When the time for bath-time arrives there can be no alternative to the packing away of toys and proceeding to the bathroom. But when it comes to deciding which toys will go into the bath today, bath-time may be more constructive from the point of view of encouraging language if he is allowed to take his choice of the kitchen strainer and funnel in place of his toy duck and steamship. 'Splash' and 'pour' can then replace 'quack-quack' and 'zoom' as the building blocks for new conversations about these objects and what you can do with them. If he is not *interested* in playing with his duck, you are wasting your time trying to get him to talk about it!

We are not suggesting that you can follow the child's lead *all* the time, or that you should, but where it can be easily fitted into the busy schedule of the care-giver, it provides the greatest opportunity for assisting your child to communicate and of encouraging his early attempts to interact with you. In sum, discover the things that interest your child, follow his lead and help him to 'talk' about them.

3   *With passive children—initiate activities that involve the child and then follow his lead.* Some children, especially those who are severely delayed in their early development, may tend to show little interest in their surroundings and may not display the exploratory behaviours characteristic of most children. In

cases like this, the care-giver's role becomes crucially important in helping to get the child interested in the everyday objects and events that make up his daily life. Parents will need to take the initiative in directing the child's attention—by activating the mobile over the child's bed, making teddy 'growl', moving toy cars and making a 'brm-brm' noise, or playing 'peek-a-boo' close to the child's face. Such stimulation will frequently obtain a reaction from the child—an outstretched hand, watching the movement, a smile or sound, and the adult can again respond to these in order to continue the interaction. Repetitive routines, such as 'peek-a-boo', 'This little piggy went to market', 'See-saw, Marjorie Daw', lifting and swinging games, are good for getting a response from children who tend to be passive. Once these routines are established and you are reliably getting a response from the child, new games can be introduced and often the child will start to initiate and ask for the game to be played. For example, if the child enjoyed being picked up and whirled round in the air, he may come and tug at your arm and stand with his arms raised, ready to be picked up. The key is to have your child as active as possible. Once the child has reached the stage of initiating, then the adult can revert to the pattern, already described, of following his lead and encouraging continued turn-taking.

Summary

A responsive, attentive, 'tuned-in' adult is the most important resource a young child can have in the early stages of acquiring his language and communication skills. It provides the child with encouragement in his early attempts at communicating and allows him to gain confidence in you, the adult, as a source of information about how to say and do new things. Learning is fun if the experience is shared with someone close to you.

So remember:
* watch closely your child's attempts to communicate and respond clearly and appropriately;
* follow his lead, rather than insisting that he does what you want;
* if he is not very active, encourage him to participate in the activities you begin but follow his lead once he joins in or

starts initiating routines and games you have shared in the past.

b) Some 'Do's' and 'Don'ts' for adults talking to young children

Many studies have shown that the way mothers talk to very young children is different from the way they talk to older children and other adults. The things they do make it easier for young children to learn the fairly difficult task of using language the way everyone else in the community uses it. Among the things mothers do are talking more slowly, using fewer words and simpler sentences and repeating the same things fairly frequently. These adjustments make it easier for the child to attend to what his mother is saying and to pick up the words that will communicate what *he* wants to say.

Some simple guidelines for talking to your child are listed below.

1 *Speak slowly and clearly*—If you speak too fast, the child may not be able to understand what you are talking about; a clear model lets him hear the words he will be trying to say.

2 *Use simple words and short sentences*—Use short, simple words to describe the objects and actions your child is involved with in his daily experiences. It may be a good idea to leave out the little words like 'a' and 'the' in the early stages, so that the child can focus on learning the main words that give him meaning. For example:

'Drink-milk', rather than 'you drink your milk'.
'Open door' rather than 'please open the door for me'.

3 *Do not talk too much*—The more you talk, the less opportunity your child has to take part in any exchange or conversation. Remember that the more a child talks, the more he learns about how to use his language. DO NOT BE AFRAID OF LEAVING SILENCES.

4 *Engage the child in joint activities*—The child's early language learning takes place through frequent repetition of familiar routines that involve shared activity and turn-taking. For example:

'Peek-a-boo' games or saying good-night to members of the family in turn.

5   *Comment on what the child says and does*—Comment in simple phrases and sentences on what your child is doing as you play together. This provides him with the language that he will need to talk about the things that interest him. Follow his lead in play rather than imposing *your* ideas on him. For example:
'Yes, wash teddy; teddy sleep; good-night, teddy.'

6   *Extend the child's language*—When talking to your child, try and provide a model for the next step that he will be taking. For example:
Child says, 'Bear eat.' You say, 'Bear eat toast.' Or child asks, 'He eat bread?' and you say, 'Yes, he's eating bread.'

7   *Do not use too many questions or commands*—If you are constantly telling the child to do things, he will be so busy trying to do what you want that he will not have a chance to talk about the things he is interested in or that he intends to do.

8   *Encourage your child when he talks*—You can do this by showing the child that you are interested in what he is telling you (even if it is hard to make him out) and by responding to what he is doing and saying. For example:
'Yes, it's a blue cup'; 'you've drunk all the milk.'

9   *Coax your child to talk more*—Sometimes when a child is hesitant, you can help him begin by giving him part of the sentence. For example:
It's a _____ (doll).
I've got two _____ (cars).

All this may seem common sense—and, indeed, it is—but it is surprising how many adults find it difficult to keep to these rules. We are so used to talking to other adults that we forget to adjust our style of talking when we are with children. A good way of knowing how well you are doing this with language-delayed children is to record a sample of your speech. We shall describe how you can do this in the next part of this section.

Conclusion

Remember that children need to hear clear models of appropriate words and have plenty of opportunities to practise using these words when they are learning to talk. The way that we talk to children is important in *all* the child's natural settings—in the home, at playgroup or pre-school, and in the wider community. It is important to remember that communication involves an interaction between the child and a key adult. The way the adult talks can make the child's task of learning to talk and even wanting to talk, very much easier.

GET SET

LISTEN TO YOURSELF TALKING

The simplest way of finding out how you talk to your child is to make a tape-recording at a time when you are playing together, or involved in some other joint activity. Tape-record five or ten minutes of your play-time together (the longer the better) and then play the tape back.

1 Listen to yourself
A common mistake adults make when playing with young children is to do too much talking. The more the adult talks,

the less opportunity there is for the child to speak. Obviously, if this happens, you will not achieve your aim of listening to children.

A good rule of thumb for adults to follow is to talk mostly:

a) *in response to what the child says*, i.e. reply to, or comment on whatever the child says, whether it is directed at you or not;

b) or to *comment on what your child is doing*.

In short, let the child do most of the initiating while you do most of the *responding*. As you listen to the playback of your session, try to identify who is doing most of the talking.

2 Analyse your language

a)   If you want to take a more detailed look at your language, we suggest that you replay the tape of the play sessions with your child but this time write out all *you* and the child said; see the example.

Draw up a form like the one shown on p. 239 and fill it in as follows:

* Take a new line for each utterance. An adult utterance can be hard to define but it is usually easy to identify in practice—pauses or silences come in between.

* If you do not have enough room on one line to write in the whole utterance, then continue on to the next line but join the lines by brackets (see example).

* The transcript should reflect the conversation that went on during the session. To do this, we use the following convention:

    Child speaks followed by adult—Utterances on same line.

    Adult speaks followed by child—Child's utterance goes on the next line.

    Child speaks, adult says nothing, child speaks—Record child's second utterance on new line; leave adult line blank.

    Adult speaks, child says nothing, adult speaks—Record adult's second utterance on new line; leave child's line blank.

    The end result is that as you read from left to right, you

follow the conversation or, more correctly, the *speaker-turns* (see example).

You will probably need more than one sheet to note down all that was said.

b)   *Why did you speak?* Go back over your transcript and, for each of your utterances, decide why you spoke and place a tick in the appropriate column. Was it because:

(i)   *Your child did something*—and you commented on it? For example, as Garret was washing the doll, Mary said, 'You wash her.' Likewise, if your child sneezed, you might have said 'Bless you.' If this is the reason, tick the column headed CHILD DID.

(ii)   *Your child said something*—and you made a reply? For instance, when Garret was feeding the doll and said, 'and mummy', Mary replied with, 'Mummy eat, yes.' If you reply to something your child both said and did—tick only CHILD SAID column.

(iii)   *You wanted to introduce the topic?*—In the previous two categories, it was the child who started the conversation. This time it was *initiated* by you. For example, when Mary knocked the cup off the table she said, 'Cup fell.' Garret did not introduce that topic. Tick the column headed MY TOPIC when you initiate something new or if you are unsure whether you spoke in response to what your child said or did.

Place only one tick against each utterance

c)   From your transcript you should now be able to derive the following totals for the whole session:

a)   Number of utterances spoken by child   ....
b)   Number of utterances spoken by adult   ....
c)   Number of times you spoke after something
      the *child did*   ....
d)   Number of times you spoke after something
      the *child said*   ....
e)   Number of times you initiated: '*My topic*'   ....

How should I talk to children?

It is impossible to give a definitive answer to that question, for

CHILD Garret   ADULT Mary   DATE 12th JAN

MY CHILD SAID	I SAID	I SPOKE BECAUSE		
		Child Did	Child Said	My Topic
	Garret look			✓
bath	Yes, dolly's in the bath		✓	
	you wash her	✓		
	get her nice and clean	✓		
bath				
dolly	dolly's in the bath		✓	
	drying dolly	✓		
dry I ?				
(chair)				
whoops				
a chair	chair, yes		✓	
a' dat	Oh yes, a tablecloth	✓		
a' dat	cup	✓		
eat	mummy eat		✓	
	We'll give her something to eat			✓
	cup fell			✓
?				
daddy eat	daddy eat, yes		✓	
and mummy	mummy eat, yes		✓	
and daddy	daddy, yes		✓	
and daddy	daddy eat, yes		✓	
and mummy	and mummy		✓	
and daddy	Oh, they must be full now they've eaten a lot haven't they?			✓
TOTAL NO. = 17	TOTAL NO. = 18 TOTALS	5	9	4

so much depends on the child you are talking to and the purpose of your session with him.

However, with a fairly talkative child, when you are concentrating on listening to his language, you should aim for:

(a)   The total number of utterances for you and your child to be much the same.

(b)   When you add the totals for 'Child did' and 'Child said', it should be higher than the total under 'My topic'.

* If this is what you did in the session with your child—well done!

* If you did *not* do it—think of why this was? Perhaps you could have another session with the child and see if you can meet these targets in that session.

Finally, cast your eyes down all the things you said. Did you use simple words and sentences? Did you ask a lot of questions or make many demands? Did you give your child lots of encouragement for talking?

It is worth repeating this activity from time to time, just to be sure that you are not developing any bad habits.

GO

CONTEXTS FOR EXTENDING CHILDREN'S LANGUAGE IN CONVERSATION

Learning to converse by gestures, sounds, single words and, finally, simple sentences, is a difficult task and can take a long time to achieve. The ways in which adults can help in all these stages has been discussed in previous chapters. But the adult's task does not end with the child's accomplishment of joining words together to form a sentence. When this stage is reached, it is vitally important to stretch and extend the child's language usage, to make sure that he is *using* his language for a wide range of purposes, in a variety of settings and with many different people. Although the foundations are achieved at home with only immediate family to 'talk' to, it is the small group or pre-school setting which is ideal for extending language skills and for ensuring that a child uses all the skills that he has learned through his close interactions at home.

The following suggestions for generating conversations are a mixture of activities that can be carried out either at home, when there are a number of children present or in a pre-school or playgroup, or during outings, such as shopping and visits to places of interest in the community. Our central message is to look for opportunities in all the child's everyday activities to extend his use of the early language skills that he has worked so hard to acquire.

a)   Interactive games and activities with groups of children

The important word is *interactive*—activities shared with or done jointly with other people. This is when children can get plenty of practice at *using* all the different types of messages that they have learnt and discover how to cope with more than just one other person. In pre-school or playgroup settings, it is important for the teachers or leaders to know what level of language skill each child has, so that they can adjust their demands on the children according to each child's abilities. This means that children functioning at quite different levels can still join together in groups for activities that are fun for all, but it ensures that the experience is beneficial to each child.

Moreover, children at immature levels get the benefit of hearing their peers using more advanced language. Some examples of group activities which are well suited to fostering communications and conversations include:

1 *Meal or snack times.* Juice or milk and fruit, sandwiches or biscuits can be available and each child has to *ask* for what he wants, at whatever level he is capable of. You may get one child pointing without making any sound; another child saying 'm' for 'milk', or 'na' for 'banana'. Yet another child may be capable of saying 'juice', 'apple' or 'want juice', 'want apple', and the most competent in the group may be able to say, I want an apple, please'. The children will benefit from the repetition and routine inherent in 'food time' and the less competent children may be 'stretched' by listening to requests modelled at more competent levels. The most important point for adults to remember is that each child's responses must be accepted at a level appropriate for him.

2 *Requesting toys.* This, too, can be done as a group activity, with the first child responding to the teacher's or parent's question. When all the children have chosen their toy, after saying first what they wanted, the teacher can ask any child which toy another child has chosen. This routine can be varied with the children taking turns at asking each other what they want and then what they have chosen. Such skills as *asking* and *answering* and *turn-taking* receive plenty of practice in this sort of situation.

3 *Greetings and 'news'.* An early morning activity common in pre-school is 'news' time. This can include 'greetings', with each child in the group greeting every other child, and any special 'news' that a child has can be shared with group. It may be a birthday, or that someone has a new puppy, or went on a visit to the zoo. Some children will require more assistance than others in 'telling' their news—a word with their parents beforehand can help to 'tune' the leaders in—but *giving information* and *sharing* one's experiences are two very important functions in communication. If telling news from home is too difficult, some objects can be placed on a mat in the centre of the circle for the children to choose, and these can form the topic of conversation for each child in turn.

4 *'Simon says' type games.* Games in which one child acts as a 'leader' and 'tells' the others what to do can be good practice for *initiating* and *demanding*. The instructions can range from copying simple motor activities, to following a sequence of commands which involve manipulating objects within the room, e.g. 'Put teddy in the pram. Put the pram in the corner'.

5 *Group games.* There can be many and varied:

a) Children can take turns holding a 'surprise bag' full of common objects, and offering it around the group in turn. The child offered the bag must put his hand in, feel an object and tell the group what it is or what you do with it before pulling it out of the bag.

b) A picture puzzle can be shared by a small group, with each child in turn picking a piece to insert but before inserting it must say what it is. Puzzles of common objects and farmyard animals are very suitable for this type of activity.

c) Picture lotto is a valuable game for a variety of language skills, and can be played by children at different levels of competence. It involves 'asking' and 'answering': 'Apple—who has apple?' and, 'I have'. It can be supplemented by having the children name the object on the card being offered, and again as it is claimed. Picture lotto comes in many shapes and forms, with pictures of widely varying objects and people—all excellent for extending vocabulary. Other make-up games can be equally effective, especially if an adult is there to model appropriate language.

d) 'Playing shop' can involve a number of children, with a pretend shop set up, and children taking turns playing the roles of shopkeepers, helper, customer. It can require *greetings*, *asking*, *answering* and *thanking*, as well as extended discussion and *commenting* about the goods for sale.

e) 'Dolly corner' games can include tea-party sequences, dressing up, bed-time routines, telephone conversations—all of which provide scope for several children to play together, taking different roles which require them to use their language in a variety of ways.

f) Similar games can be played in out-of-door settings—joint building schemes in the sandpit, with different children building parts of a car, boat or castle. Or they might share a 'tent'—either real or improvised with cardboard boxes—as a hide-out. Even simple chasing games can provide an incentive for communication.

b) One-to-one situations

We have stressed the value of one-to-one situations in children's early learning at home, but it can be equally effective in extending and stretching a child's skills in the pre-school setting, too. Leaders and helpers should allocate a certain amount of time to working with individual children in amongst the busy group situation. This enables them to check on a child's use of recently acquired skills or to plan activities and materials to teach new skills, such as plurals or adding '-ing' endings to verbs. It need not mean taking the child out of the group. For example, the leader could join the child when he is painting or working with play-dough. He could be encouraged to talk about what they are both doing. The leader should beware of other children distracting her or of moving on too quickly. She should focus exclusively on the child for at least three to five minutes at a time. It might also be worth collecting some special toys and equipment that are particularly suitable to the learning of certain language skills and use these at set times with the children who need extra help.

But it is the home setting that provides the main opportunities for one-to-one conversations that could enrich and extend the child's use of language. For instance, parents could take time to sit and watch their child's favourite TV programme with him. Do not interrupt by asking a lot of questions about what is happening, rather respond to any comments that the child makes—'yes, it *is* a pig—and extend his language by adding 'and he's eating his dinner'. Focusing on topics of joint interest gives you both opportunities to comment and will encourage your child to become more adept at descriptions. Even more valuable is the fact that you have something to talk about together after the programme has finished. Talking about things that are no longer present is a difficult skill to master, but a necessary one to encourage if your child is to be able to recount his activities to you, should you have been elsewhere when they happened.

The opportunities for one-to-one sharing at home are

many—going for walks, working in the garden together, bath-times, getting ready for bed—and all should be used for encouraging wide usage of all the language the child has acquired, and extending this gradually, in keeping with his continued growth.

c) Use symbolic material

Children's earliest understandings are learned in concrete situations, interacting with real people and real objects in their environment. As their experience extends, however, they learn that toys represent real objects and they play with them accordingly. Thus a shoe box 'becomes' a 'bed' and is so labelled. A further extension occurs when the child is able to look at pictures of real objects, and to realise that the symbol represents the real object. When this stage is reached it is very valuable to use symbolic material to extend the child's use of language. Pictures and photographs enable you to talk about familiar people, objects, actions and situations when they are not actually present, thereby extending the child's language and giving extra opportunity to practise talking about a variety of situations that are important and relevant to the child. Pictures can be chosen to 'stretch' the child's structures—to move from two words to three, to add '-ing' endings, to learn to use pronouns and plurals and past tenses. They are also useful for teaching categories of objects and for developing classification skills. A picture with mixed objects can be used for classifying into groups such as animals, fruit, tools, people.Symbolic material is thus important for elaboration and extension, and can be used in both the home and pre-school group setting.

Getting the *child* to tell stories from picture books is another way of stretching his language and communication skills.

d) Child-initiated activities

With infants, adults often have no alternative but to take an initiating role, directing their attention and encouraging the child to respond in all sorts of different ways. As children grow it becomes very important to encourage a child to *initiate*, to make choices and to place demands on others. It is an essential skill for all independent people, one that enables them to exercise control over their environment. There are many situations in which adults can encourage children to choose what *they* want to do. When playing games with objects, such as the 'surprise bag' or objects on a mat, encourage the children to choose suitable objects, to choose which games or toys they want to play with. Let children play in pairs and see that both children have a turn at organising what they will do together. Encourage them to think of actions for 'Simon says' and 'Here we go round the mulberry bush', or which story book to read.

In the home you can make changes in your routine. If you have always put the child's clothes out for him to wear in the morning, change the pattern and encourage him to get out what he needs, or to choose what toys he will play with in the bath, or take out to the sand-pit, or what game he will play with you in the evening. When you are clearing away the table, or laying it for a meal, or washing up in the kitchen, encourage your child to tell you what to do next—'spoon', 'fork', 'plate', 'cup', 'saucer'. Encourage him to look for items you need in the

supermarket—so long as you are sure you can restrain his enthusiasm for filling your basket with items you know you do *not* need! But some risks are worth taking in the cause of encouraging growing independence—and learning to initiate in many different situations is a big part of independence.

e) **Provide a wide range of experiences in different settings and with different people**
The best way of extending early language skills is to encourage children to *use* their abilities in as many different situations, and with as many different people, as possible, not in a forced way but rather as an active participant. Whenever possible, let the child speak for himself. This is easiest when visiting friends and relations, who are interested in the child and willing to be patient when communicating with an immature language user. Try to include the child in your conversations when you are shopping, visiting the doctor or health clinic and on any other special outings such as to the zoo or the park. These outings can form the basis of conversations with those at home who might not have shared the experience and provide good practice in *giving* information, and talking about sights and events experienced outside the home.

Summary
Children's language and communication skills keep growing long after they have learnt to put two or three words together to form early sentences. There are many opportunities for broadening and extending the child's language both in the home, in the pre-school and small group setting and while engaging in everyday activities with friends and relations, and out in the community.

Adults can encourage children to extend their use of language and to communicate with more and more people in an increasingly wide range of situations. Children need lots of topics to talk about and lots of opportunities to talk about them. That is how language grows—with your help.

FURTHER READING

Information about Child Development and Language

Early Language by Peter and Jill de Villiers, published by Fontana Paperbacks, London, 1979.

Baby Talk: How your child learns to speak by Susan Beck, New American Library, 1979.

The First Three Years of Life by Burton L. White, published by Avon Books, New York, 1975; W.H. Allen, London, 1979.

Young Children Learning: Talking and thinking at home and at school, by Barbara Tizard and Martin Hughes, published by Fontana Paperbacks, London, 1981.

More than Sympathy: The everyday needs of sick and handicapped children and their families by Richard Lansdown, published by Tavistock Publications, London, 1980.

The Hearing Impaired Child and the Family by Michael Nolan and Ivan Tucker, published by Souvenir Press, London, 1981. Second edition 1986.

The Secret Language of Your Child: How children talk before they can speak by David Lewis, published by Souvenir Press, London, 1978.

Introduction to Language Pathology by David Crystal, published by Edward Arnold, London, 1980.

Ideas for Activities

Let Me Play (2nd Edition) by Dorothy M. Jeffree, Roy McConkey and Simon Hewson, published by Souvenir Press, London, 1985.

The First Words Language Programme and *Two Words Together* by Bill Gillham, published by George Allen and Unwin, 1979 & 1983.

Let's Talk about It by Jean Blosser, published by Interstate Printers and Publishers Inc., Illinois, 1983.

Learning to Talk by Sandra Bochner, Penny Price and Linda Salamon, published by Special Education Centre, Macquarie University, Australia, 1984.

Helping the Handicapped Child with Early Feeding by Jennifer Warner, published by Winslow Press, Winslow, 1981.

Good Beginnings by Judith Evans and Ellen Illfield, published by High Scope Press, Michigan, 1982 (available from the National Children's Bureau, London).

Steps to Independence Series by Bruce Baker and colleagues, published by Research Press, Champaign, Illinois (various years).

Getting Through to Your Handicapped Child by Elizabeth Newson and Tony Hipgrave, published by Cambridge University Press, 1982.

Ideas for Professionals Working with Parents

Working with Parents: A practical guide for teachers and therapists by Roy McConkey, published by Croom Helm, 1985.

Involving Parents in Nursery and Primary Schools by Barbara Tizard, Jo Mortimore and Bebb Burchell, published by Grant McIntyre, London, 1983.

Parents, Professionals and Mentally Handicapped People: Approaches to partnership by Peter Mittler and Helen McConachie, published by Croom Helm, London, 1983.

RESEARCH STUDIES

Articles giving details of research studies on which this book is based

BOCHNER, S. and PRICE, P. 'Language intervention with mothers and toddlers.' In G. McIntyre and T. Parmenter (Eds.) *Preparation for Life*, 175–182, Melbourne: Prentice Hall, 1981.

BOCHNER, S., PRICE, P., SALAMON, L., and BROWNELL, M.A. 'Early Language intervention with handicapped children.' *Australian Journal of Human Communication Disorders*, December, 1981.

BOCHNER, S., PRICE, P., SALAMON, L., and BROWNELL, M.A. 'Learning to talk: An intervention program for mothers and language-delayed toddlers.' *Australian Journal of Early Childhood*, 6, 3, 1981.

BOCHNER, S., PRICE, P., SALAMON, L., YEEND, G., and ORR, E.

'Language intervention: A classroom report.' *British Journal of Disorders in Communication*, *15*, 2, 87–102, 1980.

BOCHNER, S., WARD, J., PRICE, P., and LINFOOT, K. 'Proto-linguistic behaviour in institutionalized infants.' Unpublished manuscript, Special Education Centre, Macquarie University, North Ryde, N.S.W., 2113, Australia.

CHESELDINE, S, and McCONKEY, R. 'Parental speech to young Down's Syndrome children: An intervention study.' *American Journal of Mental Deficiency*, *63*, 612–620, 1979.

McCONKEY, R. and JEFFREE, D.M. 'First steps in learning to pretend: Developing children's play.' *Special Education: Forward Trends*, *7* (2), 21–23, 1980.

McCONKEY, R., JEFFREE, D.M., and HEWSON, S. 'Involving parents in furthering the language development of young mentally handicapped children.' *British Journal of Disorders of Communication*, Vol. 4, 203–218, 1979.

McCONKEY, R., McEVOY, J., and GALLAGHER, F. 'Learning through play: The evaluation of a videocourse for parents of mentally handicapped children.' *Child: care, health and development*, *8*, 345–359, 1982.

McCONKEY, R, and MARTIN, H. 'Mother's play with toys: a longitudinal study with Down's Syndrome infants.' *Child: care, health and development*, *9*, 215–226, 1983.

McCONKEY, R. and MARTIN, H. 'A longitudinal study of mother's speech to preverbal Down's Syndrome infants.' *First Language*, *5*, 41–55, 1984.

McCONKEY, R. and MARTIN, H. 'The development of object and pretend play in Down's Syndrome infants: A longitudinal study involving mothers.' *Trisomy 21*, *1*, 27–40, 1985.

McCONKEY, R, and O'CONNOR, M. 'Implementation in the classroom of research findings on the early language development of mentally handicapped children.' *First Language*, *1*, 63–77, 1980.

McCONKEY, R. and O'CONNOR, M. 'A new approach to parental involvement in language intervention programmes.' *Child: care, health and development*, *8*, 163–176, 1982.

MARTIN, H., McCONKEY, R., and MARTIN, S. 'From acquisition theories to intervention strategies—an experiment with mentally handicapped children.' *British Journal of Disorders of Communication*, *19*, 3–14, 1984.

PRICE, P. 'A study of mother-child verbal interaction strategies with mothers of young developmentally delayed children.' Unpublished manuscript, Special Education, School of Education, Macquarie University, North Ryde, N.S.W. 2113, Australia.

PRICE, P. and BOCHNER, S. 'Issues in the teaching of language to the young intellectually handicapped child.' In J. Ward (Ed.) *Special Education in Australia.*

PRICE, P. and BOCHNER, S. 'Report of an early environmental language intervention programme.' *Australia and New Zealand Journal of Developmental Disabilities, 10,* 187–190, 1984.

INDEX